CW00868437

VOICES
OF
RESILIENCE:

Children's and Adults'
Stories of Strength & Courage of Heart

ALEX P. HARTWELL

Copyright © 2020 Alex P. Hartwell.

All rights reserved. No part of this book may be used or reproduced by any means, graphic, electronic, or mechanical, including photocopying, recording, taping or by any information storage retrieval system without the written permission of the author except in the case of brief quotations embodied in critical articles and reviews.

This book is a work of non-fiction. Unless otherwise noted, the author and the publisher make no explicit guarantees as to the accuracy of the information contained in this book and in some cases, names of people and places have been altered to protect their privacy.

Archway Publishing books may be ordered through booksellers or by contacting:

Archway Publishing
1663 Liberty Drive
Bloomington, IN 47403
www.archwaypublishing.com
844-669-3957

Because of the dynamic nature of the Internet, any web addresses or links contained in this book may have changed since publication and may no longer be valid. The views expressed in this work are solely those of the author and do not necessarily reflect the views of the publisher, and the publisher hereby disclaims any responsibility for them.

Any people depicted in stock imagery provided by Getty Images are models, and such images are being used for illustrative purposes only. Certain stock imagery © Getty Images.

ISBN: 978-1-4808-9517-1 (sc)
ISBN: 978-1-4808-9519-5 (hc)
ISBN: 978-1-4808-9518-8 (e)

Library of Congress Control Number: 2020916517

Print information available on the last page.

Archway Publishing rev. date: 12/1/2020

CONTENTS

DEDICATION

This book is dedicated to the children of the world.

They have things to say and plenty of talent for our tomorrows.

INTRODUCTION

The Topic of Resilience and How This Project Started

The theme is resilience and the goal behind this book idea is to reflect resilience stories, first from elementary school-aged students and later from adults. *"Always remember, keep your head up high. We can make it through these tough times."* One elementary school-aged student wrote this to a close friend in her class. Within a month, a chef, who along with his wife ran a catering business in the area, shared the comment that health, family, and friends are the three most important things in life. He stressed the importance of maintaining focus on things that we can accomplish, to follow through with those, and to let go of stresses we often have no control over in the first place. His example of resilient decision-making is a value for all of us.

A long-time friend, Syb, told a story from her childhood. Once her stepdad returned home from the service, her Sunday afternoon movie outing was no longer allowed. Over time, movies started to appear on television, and her parents watched movies at home on Sundays. When Syb, as an outspoken child, asked about the discrepancy between her non-movie attendance and her parents watching movies at home on Sundays, her parents did not have an answer for her. Syb used this experience in shaping a part of her own approach in life. She strives to ask and answer questions straightforwardly and is conscious of not muddying the waters with vague ideas. She gets right to the point as much as possible; this approach demonstrates a strong sense of resilience.

Encouraging a friend, prioritizing what is most important, speaking up for oneself, and making the effort to clarify your own ideas to others are examples of resilience in action. Several storytellers described one or more of these approaches and explained how these behaviors helped them.

A professional who worked with both children and young adults, all with some distress in their histories, expressed the importance of fulfilling commitments and responsibilities as part of developing resilience. His example touched on the lives of children making their way through difficulties. They need care and support; at the same time, they must learn to take responsibility regarding behaviors and boundaries. Their life's difficulties must not become crutches that foster dependence and make excuses. These difficulties best serve as an obstacle to deal with and learn from, as part of life's challenges, on the road to a productive life.

Two young adults shared a story from their junior high and high school years. They lived in a busy urban environment, questioned, and challenged their parents and teachers about everything. They became friendly with the owner of a small music store in the local area. He knew how to listen, really listen. In between normal work responsibilities, he challenged them, helped clarify and define what the kids were upset about, suggested topics to bring up at home, and ways to talk with teachers and parents. This continued for a long time and affected the lives of quite a few teens. When I heard this story, I thought of him as a 'street social worker,' or perhaps a guardian angel with invisible wings, out there teaching about resilience.

In my years as a marriage and family counselor, endless quandaries came my way. In addition to setting priorities, these quandaries included the topics of job, career, moving, starting a family, education, retirement, setting boundaries at home or at work, and taking on new adventures, among many others. Communication issues top the list. Grief processing fell into my lap right in the beginning, as an early case involved a dad with a young child coping with the tragic and unexpected death of his young wife.

My teaching experiences involved children in a variety of ages and in many different circumstances. As time went on and I continued in education, I often found that children used their own voice, spoke aloud, and expressed their questions and ideas if someone would listen. They typically displayed a positive interest in things going on around them and participated in most available activities and topics. Children need a supportive, caring environment to develop to their fullest. Even one adult in a child's life can make all the difference. After hearing and reading enough of their stories, I made it a goal to share their words with others and started writing this book. The adults I worked with and attended graduate school with at the time expressed a strong interest in this book project. Their idea was to communicate their own stories in a way that expressed how they dealt with difficulties, made tough decisions, and improved their lives. Through their stories, they hoped to encourage others.

One goal of *Voices of Resilience* is to add pieces to the puzzle about how human strength and ingenuity prevail in the face of difficulties and trauma. Resilience encompasses everything from standing back up after you have been down a long time to solving a current life problem. When challenges and trauma throw you a curve ball, resilience can start with just one action that helps you put one foot in front of the other. Friends have discussed how engaging in that one action or activity, no matter how small, helped them make choices and decisions, which gradually led to improved lives. These talks helped me understand resilience as both a learnable process and a gift.

I first read about resilience through the work of Emmy E. Werner and Ruth S. Smith, researchers who conducted a long-term study about children born and raised on the island of Kauai, Hawaii. Their book is *Overcoming the Odds: High Risk Children from Birth to Adulthood (Werner and Smith 1993, 198-202)*. They described protective factors that are important in helping an individual develop the resilience needed to rise above difficult circumstances. These protective factors include individual, inner qualities, and external supports and influences.

Through the examples in this book, it is my hope that readers will understand how individuals expressed resilience in difficult times. Learning how other people solve their own problems provides a sound step on the ladder to success for those who are facing difficulties, making hard decisions, or want to develop and display resilience.

Special Note: The author changed all the storytellers' names and paraphrased most stories to protect privacy. Notarized permission was obtained from some storytellers to use their own words.

ONE

Children's Messages to Family, Friends, and Professionals: Ideas on Values, Gratitude, and Friendship

C hildren have touching things to say to adults in their lives. They tell them how to live, which attitudes are worth developing, how to behave, and how to treat children and each other. The children describe what they like and do not like in direct terms. Their words speak clearly for themselves and resilience shines through. The children raise issues and sometimes have the answer ready.

Cole wrote live life for real and not for just your best wishes about it. We have to keep going and trust that we will find our way. Think first and act later. Let mistakes teach you something. Love those around you, be respectful, and learn from each other.

Doug wrote to his dad. He told him he loves those new shoes, and said thanks again. His school progress is good; they can both be happy about that. Doug's plan is to have a great job once he is old enough and finishes all his schooling. He would like to switch schools but that is just not happening right now. Doug told his dad that he misses him.

Doug will see his grandmother soon, hopefully right after that haircut he mentioned earlier. He will help mom move furniture around to make room for Grandma, and it will be great for all of them!

Doug's strongest message is for his dad to not do drugs or hang out with those friends who live that way. Be healthy and stay well. Doug told his dad that he loves him a lot.

Josh wrote that someone who is a good friend might know you for ages and ages. You are kind and caring toward each other. It does not matter whether you are just sharing a pizza or solving a big problem. It goes both ways; you trust each other and you can depend on each other. If it came down to it, your friend would tell you to stay off drugs and stay out of trouble.

Jerilyn wrote to her former teacher. She sent him a wish that things were going well for him. She went on to say that she was fine in her new school, getting good grades, but she does miss them, all of them. She asked him to say hi to everyone for her. She is about to grow out of the grades he normally teaches! That did not seem possible.

Jerilyn loves that teddy bear they sent! Its new name is J and it sits on her bed pillow every day. Jerilyn said that she has gotten acquainted with some of the folks at her new school. She was kind of mad at her teacher the other day, but then she got over it. The teacher is okay. Jerilyn plans to have a talk with her again to help her teacher understand her. Jerilyn is confident that they will do okay after a while. Most of the kids like her a lot, so she can't be all bad!

It takes time with that illness her mom and dad talked about, and that's the hardest thing for sure. Some church people help folks who need help. She is acquainted with them and watches how they work. They are especially nice and Jerilyn hopes they stay in her life for a long time.

Jerilyn included some of her work, along with her letter, for him to see. She also included a painting and if there's room, she planned to add in a few other things. She ended with a request that he write back when he can, and said that she plans to visit all of them one of these days.

Margret wrote about her grandparents. She expressed gratefulness because they are around whenever she needs someone. They make themselves available. They help with problems. She wonders what she would ever do without her grandparents and expresses confidence that it is not a worry; they are there for her in both the best and worst times of her life.

Joseph's message is for parents to let kids enjoy playtime before starting homework. Don't be pushy about it; let homework wait a while. They will use excess energy outdoors, enjoy daylight, and start homework later. Snacks would be good as long as they don't run around and choke on them. They should not ruin their teeth either. That's it for now. Bye.

Tressa shared that school was going well. She expected to finish college and become a pediatrician by age 41, possibly sooner. Science fiction books are a favorite, and she plans to read her teacher's upcoming book. Tressa likes to share her thoughts on life with others.

Alena wrote home that it hurts how much she misses her mom. Alena says it is unbelievable how much she loves her mom. She goes on to say she especially loves it when her mom laughs and tells Alena that she loves her! Alena reported that her tummy hurts at times and ended with a comment that her new friends are fun to be around and they tell great ghost stories.

Brieann wrote that people should respect each other. It makes things difficult when people are mean instead of nice to each other. They could get along instead of fighting, facing war, or have rapes and killing happen in our country.

Things are not perfect or the way she wants them to be. As God made all people, her advice is that we should try to act better in the first place. Brieann would like to make it so people did all right together, were happy enough, and worked to come up with solutions to problems.

When she is older, she wants to be well known enough to help others make a good life for themselves and for those around them.

She ended by saying have a great day and thanked each person for reading her words.

Amber wrote to the counselor. She likes it so much that her counselor is around and working to help her as part of that after-school program. She said that the questions asked by the counselor help her and the rest of the kids think about things better. The counselor understands their educational goals and helps them get clear about what they want in other ways too. Amber likes how the counselor listens and treats her well, just the way she wants her to.

Amber went on to say that her suggestions are great and do help. The counselor knows how to make Amber feel better, and she doesn't get mad just because Amber gets mad sometimes.

Amber wants her counselor's boss to give her extra time off for doing such a good job!

Teddy remembered about his grandma. Home and love, love and home, no matter where home really is, or how it changes at times, the two go together. When Grandma died, he sobbed and cried. She was love and we felt at home together every visit. He wrote that when he talked it over with his mom, he told the truth. Teddy told her how he felt. He told her that he loves her, to remember Grandma, and to keep prayers going every day.

Jeremy wrote that his life was typical. His parents lived apart and he did not want to be around his dad. They moved pretty often. His grandma took care of the family when his mom left for work, and even though his grandma had cancer, she did all right for a long time. What he wanted to share is that it is wise to learn to get along with others, just do your best every day. What you send out into the world comes back to you. It could haunt you. Pay attention to this idea.

Mackenzie wrote to his counselor that this essay is to thank him for his help, especially from the other day. Our house had so much damage from that storm; his mom had to get help. There was no way to fix it otherwise. Helpers did a lot of work, and Mom was so grateful. She took photos of before and after, just so they would remember what they went through together. Mackenzie appreciated his counselor's extra support and his special effort for his mom. He was sure that they would all have a good visit together and ended his note with thanks again, a smiley face, and good-bye.

Jessica wrote a hello note to her former teachers. She had been thinking about them, and asked how they were doing. Jessica told them that she has been having a great time at her new school. She thanked them for bringing all those books and magazines. That was so special because it was from them! She liked the hugs too!

One new friend has become a close friend already. This feels good to her. They share a lot, even their feelings; they know how to make each other feel better. They laugh together.

It means a lot that these teachers still keep in touch and Jessica thanked them again.

Philip wrote about careers. Philip said he would work hard to succeed and do a super job of being a doctor. He would keep patients and their relatives close to his heart. His goal was for success and improvements as needed. Future patients would want to come back to him, to develop friendly relationships with him, and he said he would help all who come to him.

Philip expected his friend Nicholas and himself to become well known. Their goal was to help poor and rich alike. Their work would reflect a strong education from a top medical school. Besides good grades, they would complete projects for different charities. They would work to help people have enough food and not have pain and suffering. Another goal was to build a hospital that takes in every person without fail.

Philip read a science book at home, which talked about doctors and medicine, and that was where the idea for medical school originally came from. His life was rough at the time. His family had problems and they had to solve some of those. He hoped that all of it would work out all right. He had confidence, especially in his dad. His dad would correct any problems and take care of things. Philip remained hopeful through all of these problems.

Philip expressed confidence about his ability to accomplish these goals. He believed the training would be excellent and that he had enough talent to help with healing and fixing problems. His dad gave him encouragement about choosing any goal and then setting out to make it work. Whatever Philip goes for, his dad has faith that he will succeed in that field. Philip concluded with a comment that his and Nicholas's story is about the very best doctors around.

Greg wrote that his counselor treated him really well, just the way the counselor would want to be treated. His counselor was caring and helpful, and he shared special art projects with Greg that they worked on together. Greg went on to say that his counselor was seeing to it that he returned home as soon as possible. It was up to doctors and the surgeon too, but Greg hoped his counselor could influence the doctors. Greg has a large extended family and favorite pets, including one parrot, a dog, and colorful fish that he feeds every day. He wants to see them all and can't wait for the next cookout!

Jamal wrote to a friend. He misses him a lot. No one understands him the way this friend does. He tries to explain to newer friends so they will get it, but it's not like when he and his old friend talk. He just can't wait to see him again!

Caitlin wrote to a close friend. She misses this friend already! Caitlin told her that she's been such a good friend to her. Let's plan to stay friends wherever we live, she wrote. Be brave through all your challenges and know you will be okay. Know that we both will.

Kirstyn wrote that her mom received faulty information, some of it not even true. The counselor just absolutely has to clear it up and not be involved with something that might be a lie. Then Kirstyn went on to thank her counselor for the visits back and forth. Kirstyn said the counselor is okay even though sometimes she gets mad at her. She thanked the counselor for helping her out when she is not doing well.

Kevin wrote about his grandmother. Gramma is so good to him. She is sweet as she can be. They bake cookies together filled with chocolate chips and raisins and nuts. They are so yummy! When he feels sad, Kevin can sit on her lap and that makes him feel better. She listens to his stories and then tells him her own stories.

Elsie wrote that people should strive to be better than they were; they should follow the rules. Stay away from drugs and stay out of trouble. To be better means they should stop making poor decisions, learn to make better ones, and actively care about others.

Dylon wrote to thank his grandmother for giving him advice, asking good questions, listening to what he said, and letting him ask questions too. She was helpful to him. In addition, she did things for the family and helped him figure out things about his own life. Dylon said he feels better when he talks things out with her.

Lorenzo wrote to ask his mom to bring him some photos and other things. He wanted to return home soon and asked her to take care of it. He mentioned that he and his sister would attend court together, and they would call her as soon as they could.

Will wrote that parents should be appropriate in how they treat their children. If the child needs discipline, grounding would be all right. Beating them up is not all right. This happens too often and it should stop. Parents need to work to improve their own behaviors. Children need plenty of attention to grow and learn; they need to play and have many activities. Parents could arrange the family's schedule in ways that are more productive. Will ended by saying parents could practice to do better all around.

Jennifer wrote to her aunt that she did not know how to answer her aunt's questions right away over the phone. Jennifer mentioned that she needs extra time to be able to express thoughts or questions, and she is working on this in class too. She went on to tell her aunt that she really liked the cake and ice cream her aunt brought on that last visit. It was yummy!

Carina wrote a story about treating people well. Her message is that people need to relearn about discipline, whether it applies to themselves, their children, or other people. Abuse should not happen; people should treat each other better in the first place. In addition, people in general do not pay enough attention to realize that others are mistreated. They have to realize there is abuse going on, and then they need to work to make a positive change in society.

There is too much discrimination, and the very people who should listen closely often do not. This includes families, human services, the courts, as well as politicians and others of high rank in society.

Students do not go to teachers often enough to report something bad, sometimes to avoid increased bullying that would likely come their way. Teachers have to see what is really going on. Then they should work to fix it.

Carina ended with an encouragement for adults to find that one steady tiny light in the dark tunnel; when one light does not stay lit, maybe the next one will. If people looked and thought more carefully, they could make the world better for us and for later generations.

Emily wrote to her counselor to say thanks for all the things the counselor did for her. She especially mentioned the hope and wish that the counselor would be able to return Emily to her family.

Hunter wrote and thanked the staff at the activity center for not making a big deal out of his moments of mischief. He thanked them for their overall support. His family was moving due to his dad's job. He also sent a note to his teachers to thank them for their help with schoolwork. He wished everyone good luck in the future.

Lani wrote that her pen name is Josie. She stated she was doing well, working hard in school, and planned on a career after college. She and a classmate talk a lot about these ideas. One goal is to work toward bettering her life every day. She thanked her teacher for inquiring about her thoughts and letting her share these ideas with others.

Selene shared her top three wishes. One was for her family to be reunited, that peace existed in every country, and that her genie could run around free every day.

Various children made comments about the risk of war and our country ever going to war. Logan said we should always use our best army; our army has to be its best or it would be just too scary. No one wants to get shot. Almira said that most children would say stop war. Stop it for good. Otherwise, too many family members will die and too many people will cry and feel hurt. Nate, as a young Marine, requested that the president write to him. Mack wrote about God's blessings on our country and each of us. We should keep Jesus in our hearts. He invited the president to visit. Natalie wrote that in her heart she knew our country would survive with pride and dignity. Our flag will fly.

TWO

CHILDREN'S STORIES ABOUT CHANGING ENVIRONMENTS

C hildren who are in a temporary shelter for any reason often face living arrangement and school location changes. In listening to their comments and curious questions, and in reading the stories and poems they wanted to share, it became obvious that they had clear ideas about what they understood, as well as about what they would like to see happen in the short term and later on in their lives. The feelings expressed ranged from worry and concern to acceptance and excitement. They wondered how they would get along with their classmates, how much recess time would be allowed, whether classes would be easier or harder than the current ones, if their new teachers would like them. Typically, they hoped to return home, whether with their original family, relatives, or a newfound family.

Clark wrote about concerns. He was worried about his mom and wondered how long he would have to be away from her. How long do comas last? His dad said he could see her whether she wakes right up or not. His hope is that she wakes right up; a day or two more would be okay. He is still doing all right in school and hopes to have a long visit with his friends one day soon.

Lance wrote about moving away pressures. He is on the quiet side. Would new classmates try to get along with him okay? Would they talk with him or just talk about him? Then there are his friends here. It's hard to think about living somewhere else. His old friends would not be there with him. That would be the strange part. His wish is that he could just stay put until he is totally grown up. Then it would be fine to move away. One of his ideas is to become an artist and live in Europe. His house there would be large and well equipped. It would be most important, Lance concluded, for him to take care of his family.

Anthony wrote that his idea is to get home to his family. He and his sibling were in foster care for a while, which did not work out well for them. They felt picked on by the other kids and felt no one cared. The siblings are together again right now and expect a reunion with their whole family soon.

Kimberly wrote this message. The place she has been staying at turned out okay, which really surprised her. It seemed so awful that first day. Now she's made new friends and gets along well with everyone. It is almost time to start over. How will she fit in? Kimberly wishes she could stay put and remain here for a long time.

She will miss everyone. Some adults here are her favorites in the whole galaxy. Her two best friends are here too. For now, the best they can do is write letters and keep in touch that way.

Jackson wondered what it would be like with a foster family. He wondered if they would like him or not. Would he be able to live with his aunt? What would happen if he could not see his parents? New kinds of food would be awful. His siblings may or may not be able to come with him, and he was always concerned about them. He wondered what it would be like to live in a different state. Jackson's bottom line, and what had been on his mind every day, was how many more days were there until he would get home?

THREE

CHILDREN'S STORIES OF GHOSTS, GOBLINS, AND LETTING OFF STEAM

These stories emerged during a period when various individuals, or small groups of children, wrote or recorded stories from their imaginations. I had quite a selection and chose these to help the reader see another side of the children and to allow the children to tell about one of their ways of "letting off steam."

Joshua told the story of rowing down the stream with his mom. All was well until he dunked his head too far under the water and his mom screamed at him. His next mistake was fooling around with the paddle instead of rowing properly. The anaconda he came up with, totally by accident, landed on his shoulder and freaked them both out. Somehow, as the anaconda opened its mouth wide, they managed to knock it back into the water. That was when Joshua realized this was a dream and decided it would be even better to call it a scream dream.

Marisol told this story about a fun and scary time. We had a fun trip to Hawaii. We were taking baths quite late one night and crashed out rather quickly after that. Something woke us up in one of our rooms; it looked like a corpse running along the wall. That wall looked scratched and we heard a combination of yelling and growling noises. Sharla made no noise at all and Allie made lots of noise while they both watched. They got up and out of bed to share stories together. Suddenly, something was lying on the bed right next to where Allie had been. It looked like a person but then it looked like a ghost. Sharla saw its two white eyes staring at her. She worried too much to go tell one of the adults in our party about this. Instead, Sharla ran to our adjacent room, woke us up, and told us every detail. We decided that it was definitely a ghost.

Another night the ghost reappeared. I saw it this time. I did not bother with listening for noises or watching it move. I screamed like crazy and two adults from our party came in. It looked like they thought I overdid it, or maybe I had a bad dream. Later I talked about it with a therapist. I described every detail as best I could. The therapist dismissed it as bad dreams indeed. That, of course, was not true. It was never about bad dreams.

On our last day, we had a downpour. We ran quickly to the car and flew home with no trouble. We slept at one of our houses that first night back. Spirits started to show up again, danced around the walls, and at first looked even worse. We remembered some chants, said Jesus's name, and then those spirits, or ghosts, disappeared. We never saw them again. They never returned.

Together, Tasha and Tyler told this story about vampires.

The little boy did not like it when his mother reminded him that he was on restriction and not allowed to go to the park. A short visit with his friend in their yard would be fine. When his friend suggested playing in the park, the little boy said no at first. He couldn't go or there would be trouble at home. After a while, they went anyway. He knew his mom would be angry, but he and his friend had fun together. While they walked through the park, they saw a strange-looking man.

The man looked mean and scary. The two boys did not know it, but this man could become something else just by thinking about it. The boys played together and had fun. Soon the man walked close to them. The friend who should not have been there asked the other friend what the man wanted. The other friend told him he worries too much and the man would not bother them. The man then asked if the boys' moms knew where they were. When they said no, they accepted the man's offer to let them use his phone to call them. The boys went with him and once they were in his house, he told them he had them now and shouted that he had fooled them.

Both boys were scared. What if he hurts us; he might eat us for dinner! What we should do is get out of here! The boys talked together—how to do that, how to escape? One of their moms was already looking for them. She thought of them playing at the park first thing, so she started walking through it. The vampire man's house was within sight of the park, and the boys started screaming for her the moment they saw her. She realized what happened and came up with a plan to fool the vampire and get both boys out of there. The mom succeeded. At home once again, it was time to let everyone know that a vampire had moved in and lived close to the park. Beware of vampires.

Jesse shared a scary story about death. Everyone started to die at the local carnival. People dropped like flies. She just about flew out of there and ran to the police station. She saw people sprawled on sidewalks along the way; at the station, everyone looked dead. Jesse appeared to be the only person still alive. She then died in her nightmare, woke up, and ran to find her mom.

FOUR

CHILDREN'S STORIES FROM THE HEART

These from-the-heart stories touch deeply to the core of each writer. Writers reveal humor and courage of heart. They show relief when something positive happens, as in the story that ends with a comment about a child getting a new mom. Resilience shines through each one of these stories and reflects determination, grit, and confidence about upcoming improvements in life.

Ginger wrote about deep inside places that provide emotional comfort. Sometimes something goes wrong. She feels bad; she feels just awful. It is too much. That's when she leaves here, the outside world, and travels below the surface. Ginger keeps her happy thoughts there decorated with flowers and beautiful colors. The music is soothing. No one knows about this place. She keeps it to herself. It is for her to visit whenever things get too heavy to handle. It is a place of recovery and restoration. It helps her cope every day.

Janine wrote these words on friendship and hidden hurts. She just never realized that you could hurt so much from bruises that no one sees. That scars are there; no one knows where they came from or even that they are there. They are invisible. These wounds wind up hurting a lot and can do real damage. Janine just learned that this is why a certain person in her class sometimes walks away, stays to herself, so quiet. Janine might be able to help; she can at least reach out and be a friend. That is what she has just learned.

Natalie wrote a story about a girl named Carol Ann. Carol Ann never knew her own parents. If someone asked about them, Carol Ann withdrew and did not say much. She was really mad at them for leaving her with her grandmother even though she loved her grandmother. This grandmother, in Carol Ann's mind, treats her the way moms should always treat their children. Carol Ann did not realize it until later, but her mother worked to save Carol Ann's life by having her move into her grandmother's house.

Carol Ann's grandmother was a good cook, and she shared plenty of stories. But she would not talk about Carol Ann's parents. Later, Carol Ann thought that to talk about her parents would make her grandmother feel down and sad. Carol Ann knew there were medicines at her parents' home, worried calls to doctors, and constant money troubles. Sometimes it was just too much.

Grandmother's stories were personal ones about life when she was Carol Ann's age, and they were fun stories to hear. They were even more fun when her grandmother revealed how she got into a bit of trouble now and then. Carol Ann laughed a lot while she listened. This made them both feel good.

This is Katelin's story. It happened on Christmas Eve. Her dad rushed her mom to the hospital while Katelin's grandparents took care of her and her siblings. Her dad said he barely got the car door opened when the baby just about popped right out. Katelin's dad ran to get a wheelchair and put her mom in it. They made it inside the hospital door and an attendant moved her mom into a bed as quickly as he could. A man dressed as Santa put the baby in a big stocking and said, "Merry Christmas," as he handed the stocking to her mom. Mom decided on the spot that the baby's name should be Noelle. Things have worked out well since then. Katelin's mom said they had enough children at that point, but Katelin and her siblings hope for one more—a boy for their older brother, the only boy in the family.

Ray wrote about his family. He wrote that his mother went through quite a lot in recent years. They went driving around together early one morning when his mom thought someone had snuck into their house. It worked out okay. He wanted to live with his dad and grew tired of going back and forth all the time. His hope remained a hope at this time.

Ray wrote that no one understands what goes on inside him. No one knows his own pain and bad feelings. It was difficult to talk about this with his friends, but he did sometimes. He could also talk to one particular school counselor. It was not easy in either case.

His wish is for other people to lead normal, healthy lives. If bad things happened in their earlier lives, it is important to make double sure not to treat their own children that same way. They should treat them with love and respect. Discipline is okay but not abuse. They should never treat children or other people badly.

Hope was the one thing that helped Ray during his hard times. He wrote that hope is one of the best gifts that one person could give another, especially when someone is feeling down. Hope is a treasure, along with acts of kindness. Even small acts of kindness mean a lot. Both of these things helped Ray a lot when he really needed help.

Ray was right about his dad. He and his dad reunited and after a while, his dad met a caring and lovable woman who would soon become Ray's stepmom. Ray wrote that he is happy and so relieved now.

Kenisha and friends told this story. Missionaries adopted some children after their parents became too ill to care for them. They did have to move around for a short time and attend different schools; eventually, they settled down in one neighborhood. Some of their earlier caretakers did not like to see them cry when a child left or when a close friend moved away. Because of that, the children were not allowed to say good-bye.

Things got better with the missionaries. Their message for the reader is that the missionaries let them say hello and good-bye, whenever change happened, with everyone they met. Missionaries did not try to protect them from their own feelings. They taught them to accept their feelings. At the same time, they taught them to wish people well and then get right back to the task of continuing with their own lives. They defined hellos and good-byes, even when it hurts sometimes, as a normal part of life. Kenisha and her friends thought this was the best way to be.

Camille wrote about how adults should live. She first wrote that with all the misbehaviors in the world, including drinking, smoking, and robberies, people could stop mistreating children. That is step one. Abuse is not all right; it just never is. Her goal is for this story to become part of an information book.

Camille wrote that a difficult thing happened in her family when she was still a preschooler. Late one night she heard loud noises like glass smashing to bits. A car door slammed as she and her siblings looked out the window. Mom cried. Dad left home, left their mom, herself, and her siblings. All at once, he just drove away. They hugged their mom and just held each other.

The next part of the story took place in a foster home where she was harassed at times by one of her foster brothers. She wondered about God letting this happen, and then she decided it was not His fault. It was just life. She left that foster home and found a different place to live.

Camille believes that we can all work to make life better for ourselves, for each other. If we work hard enough in our own lives with better choices, life will improve all the way around. That is what she wanted to say.

P.S. Do two things to make life better—less booze, less weed and pot. She wanted to thank you for reading this message.

FIVE

Gus
"Finding My Way"

One main turning point in Gus's life was that he sustained a serious knee injury that forced him to rethink career choices and goals. Gus was working with students at the time of this story.

Gus's opening comment was that he had no career inclinations during his high school and early college years. His energy was somewhere else. He did not apply himself and remained without focus. General education course requirements were complete and that was about it. He and a new friend started playing basketball together. Gus's natural ability for basketball showed up every time they played. He credits this friend with helping him make such an important connection.

Gus did not want to let himself down, or disappoint his parents, which he believed would come next. Picking a major was a challenge. Nothing fit well. Gus continued to have trouble with classes and chalked it up to immaturity. Pressure increased because a girlfriend started at the same school, and he needed to talk to his parents about his confusion, difficulty with classes, and lack of a major. Success in life meant taking action on his part; there is no doubt about this.

Once he restarted classes, Gus took one class to build his confidence, and then he signed up for two. Belief in having abilities became possible. A girlfriend talked about her interest in opening a childcare center, while other friends had recently started a recreation center. Gus had a good feeling about both projects, and he felt some confidence about his opportunities to participate. He got along well with younger children and started taking early childhood development classes; he liked this area well enough to declare it a major.

Little by little, a solid path became clearer. With general education out of the way, and high grades in early childhood courses, success was within reach. Basketball continued to be a part of life, and that first basketball tournament turned out to be a fun challenge. It was time to further his life's plan; he was now in his mid-twenties. Through his early college years, Gus worked in the dietary department at a local hospital. He graduated college while he was in his late twenties, and he remained in the same job the whole time. A local university accepted him for a bachelor's program that involved somewhat older children. He and his parents were proud of this achievement—it meant something to the whole family. Gus knew what it meant to his parents to watch his progress, as they did not have those opportunities at his age.

Gus had one lifelong goal that re-emerged during his time at the university. He succeeded in an emergency medical technician (EMT) course, a basic requirement for any work involved with the fire department, which was an early dream job. Once Gus finished this course, the job assignment at the hospital changed from the dietary department to the emergency room (ER). Gus made friends with various students who attended class with him. One close friendship developed with a professor of an organization and management class.

A local elementary school offered Gus an internship, which he could use to complete a requirement for the undergraduate program. The classroom Gus worked in functioned so well that it triggered him to look into a teaching career. Both the principal and teachers gave him encouragement toward that profession. They recognized some of Gus's abilities in that direction and thought a classroom would work out just fine for him.

A lot of pride ran through the family on graduation day. The EMT work was full time for Gus now. Riding along in an ambulance with a fellow EMT was one aspect of this job, though the hospital atmosphere provided a greater learning opportunity. He developed a lot of respect for nurses, especially in how they handled their work. He assisted them with basic things, such as bandages and heart rates. At that time, he did not do blood draws. He took electrocardiograms (EKGs) and saw to restocking necessary items. Gus found a tender spot within himself whenever he encountered an elderly patient.

His next assignment was in cardiopulmonary resuscitation (CPR). Gus had an interesting story to tell about his early CPR experiences. The person in charge invited Gus to get right in on it, full steam ahead. Gus hurried into the room with a young victim. The second he entered the room it was as if everything stopped. Silence surrounded him. This was Gus's first real-life experience with CPR, and the medical personnel looked right at him. This nonstop CPR procedure continued until doctors determined that the patient did not make it. It was freaky when that determination was made, because Gus heard that this healthy-looking young man simply fell over while outdoors. He had mixed feelings even though he knew that a full-blown heart attack outside the hospital leaves only a remote chance of survival regardless of age. That young a death, in addition to the fact that it was his first CPR case, bothered him for some time.

A small number of duty shifts for CPR came and went for Gus, and no patient survived. CPR uses teamwork as opposed to individual work; even so, the deaths still disturbed him. Medical coworkers added in some humor as part of these early experiences for Gus, telling each other to watch out for "Doc Demise" whenever he walked into the room. The next day, the patient survived. What a relief that was! Watching life and death close up like this does affect people. For Gus, how short life is became a strong message.

Becoming a firefighter and teaching school were on Gus's mind once graduation was over. He had his own place to live, took on responsibilities, and felt good about his life's direction. Two local hospitals sponsored a basketball game; a coworker invited him to play. The impression during the first part of the practice session was that he should be able to handle this level okay. Gus believed he would not need to play full strength and would only need practice and timing improvement.

He sustained a serious injury toward the end of basketball practice. It was his knee, which he felt and heard at the same time. He went to the ER and once the swelling was gone, he recovered quickly. He played again and wrecked the knee again. In this weakened state, Gus's knee gave out and routinely swelled.

Surgery came into Gus's life—basketball and fire departments went out. Gus knew that fire departments pick people who are strong and in good shape. Neither field can use a person with weak knees. Even with a routine surgery, there is still a chance for a glitch, which concerned Gus and made him nervous.

The machines used right after surgery, plus the physical therapy a little later, were extremely painful. Physical therapy caused Gus to feel faint at first. Driving was out of the question; friends and family helped him get to appointments. The apartment no longer worked for Gus. The combination of extended therapy and restrictions on day-to-day movement resulted in him leaving hospital work for a time. There was no shortening of the healing process in this particular case—it took several months.

Gus was able to return to work as an EMT and thought about alternative options within fire department work. The fire department idea remained in his mind's eye; daydreams occurred about what type of unusual role might develop, or a connection through networking might bring the fire department goal to life. Gus decided that although he gained immensely in so many ways from the work and training, it was time to leave the hospital and find other employment.

Specialized work with children came into view, in particular children who were seriously ill; whose families needed help with different issues. Gus inquired about work with juvenile delinquents and discovered another children's program to explore. The age range for that program suited him, and the counseling used fit his personality. Childhood education training and successful classroom experience added to his application. He was a better fit for this program than in the program for the older students. Relating to younger children suited him quite well.

Gus's optimistic and upbeat nature helped in his work with children. Talking with them was easy for him, and the variety of activities involved was enjoyable. Children taught him more than all his classes combined. Becoming aware of who the children were, which mentoring topics proved most useful, and how to help them make good decisions for their futures intrigued Gus immensely. There were additional beneficial effects for him as well—this experience expanded his education tremendously.

Gus continued exploring future careers and future goals. Several areas opened to him, and it became necessary to include financial considerations in with all the rest. The financial goals part was essential in order to meet future objectives. Gus hoped to gain experience as a substitute teacher and somehow mix that with his current position. He started looking into master's degree and credential programs in the field of education. Gus expressed excitement about these opportunities, and he acknowledged the need to investigate the details further. He kept moving forward.

Gus's ability to share the development of certain ideas and boundaries along the way helps to shed light on one way that problem-solving tools develop. He used a one-thing-at-a-time approach for some issues and was willing to explore other issues in more depth. His curiosity and humor, even when faced with difficulties and disappointments, also display resilience.

Annie
"Strict Attention"

One boundary for Annie was learning to restrict involvement in sports programs in college. Another was learning to speak up more clearly for herself in the work environment. As a young adult, Annie worked with children on a daily basis. She engaged them in baking activities, arts and crafts projects, walks and exercise programs, as well as homework completion during after-school hours.

Annie's dad worked as a physician and after one son, he looked forward to raising a daughter. He expected someone quiet and playful; instead, he got one who was squirrelly and bouncy. He knew his daughter would need structure at an early age more than his son ever did. It was a thrill for him nonetheless. He and his wife set about with their new larger family in tow and carried on with their normal child-rearing plans.

Annie chuckled as she shared this part of the story. A high IQ proved to be an advantage. Schoolwork came easy and she developed a strong memory. This helped balance out a lack of focus that occurred at times. Annie thought she was just like everyone else while going through childhood. Success in school continued. In elementary school, report card comments said she was a pleasure to have in class, and along with high grades, the next comment said 'disrupted others at times.' Annie knew how to get along in class and play well with others during recess. On the home front, Annie's dad wound up helping her mom to understand Annie. She never truly heard her mom's request for help—an everyday example was kitchen chores. A typical response was yes. She would do what her mom asked, but she never really heard the request. With some effort, the family found a way to resolve this to everyone's satisfaction.

Annie did not realize she was the one typically shouting out answers as a youngster. No one walked past the classroom door without Annie's observation. She started to notice contradictions during high school. She could not contain classroom questions until the appropriate time. Social skills came naturally to Annie, a definite high school and lifelong benefit, yet high school friends could wait their turn. These observations raised quandaries for Annie, but she kept them inside.

Annie expressed gratitude many times throughout this story. The caring and reinforcement her parents routinely gave their children made a difference in later life. Earlier, Annie thought every family lived this way; as she got older, she realized this was not the case. She learned so much about what is important in life, principles to maintain, and respect. She believes this could only have come from them. Annie credits both parents for her capacity to accomplish and set goals today. Even in high school, they let her find her own way. She did make mistakes, but her parents were around as needed to help make things right. Independence in thinking and action were encouraged.

Annie next discussed a couple of major events. First, as a high school junior, the temptation to ditch school a couple of times proved too much to resist. Annie's grades were high. Her parents were not expecting to hear the announcement that she spent the school day at the beach. They were flabbergasted, and they really had no idea what to make of it. This behavior never became a habit on Annie's part, for which the family remained grateful.

Here is the second incident. Annie told her parents as a high school senior that she would rather forget college, move somewhere, and explore life. Travel as part of high school sports led her to believe this would be the best thing after graduation. Her parents had various responses. The first response was that it was perfectly A-OK to have a good adventure, as long as she could pay her own way. This included covering travel expenses, apartment rental, groceries, health insurance, car, and phone. Support would end the day she left. Next, that well-known-to-parents-globe-wide 'Riot Act' delivered in 'No Uncertain Terms' comprised their response. They let her know exactly what they thought of moving away with no job prospects and no college education behind her. Annie could tell they thought she had lost her mind.

Her parents continued with a reminder about her college acceptance letter. The option was for Annie to go to school full time with tuition and basic expenses fully paid for the whole four years. She would not have to work at all during the school year, although a summer job was a requirement. Annie was glad she came back to her senses in time!

College is often where the challenges begin for some students. Annie was concerned about some aspects of it. One example was those mandatory four-hour classes. Her dad knew that although it was easy to breeze through school up to this point, Annie did not always pay close attention. He described medication for them to look into together to help with college. Annie's pride and stubbornness kicked in to create an alternate approach. The choice was to grit her teeth, meet class challenges head on, and just do the work. This approach fully gained her dad's support. He dropped the research and medication idea altogether.

Annie did have to push to make it through classes. The sports activity of her first semester typically took up four hours a day just for practice. Her participation did not last long because class studies required so much time. It was simply not possible to delay or put off various academic tasks and still do okay. Failure was not an option in her perfectionistic mind's eye. This amount of effort eventually caught up with Annie, and it presented health challenges that required medical treatment for one term. Minor health issues occurred now and then in high school and the family thought there might be a connection. She did take care of her health, though, and soon returned to normal. Her parents objected when they learned that, at all times, studies had to come before fun activities could start. They wanted to see her relax a bit and take a breather, balance things a little differently, and make sure she stayed well. Annie carried on in her usual determined manner.

Over time, one change did happen. Concern for other people kept her from developing assertiveness for a while, even though speaking up with family and friends at a young age had been easy. As a newly employed young woman, Annie tried to protect other people's feelings by remaining on the quiet side. Once involved in childcare work, however, she learned to speak up for herself. This included speaking up with children and staff, as well as the administration. It was either speak up at times or perish on the spot!

Annie's parents maintained a well-balanced approach throughout child-rearing years. They taught Annie and her brother about hard work, money, and leisure. They offered a good combination of structure and tolerance for behaviors. They encouraged education, curiosity, taught their children to explore for their own futures, and to respect others. Church was routine for the family.

Annie recognized her family for their support, the freedom they allowed, the structure and framework of her young life, and even the consequences she did not want to hear at any given moment. All these aspects of upbringing contributed to perseverance, success with goals, and the ability to overcome all obstacles she encountered.

Garrett
"Small Town Life"

Garrett held administrative positions over a large number of years, and he maintained a positive attitude and approach toward everyone he encountered, whether child, teacher, staff member, or another administrator.

Garrett started out talking about childhood with several siblings. Blessings and challenges were involved. While in junior high, his parents divorced. He still lives by the values he learned back then and credits his mom and grandmother for those endless lessons. Love and caring were a prominent part of early family life. Knowledge of and confidence in their love was obvious at all times. His dad had no siblings, and his mother came from a small family. All four grandparents were in his life for a number of years.

Willingness to do his current work, and love for his own family, is a direct result of the loving environment of Garrett's early childhood. The goal to provide well, both at home and at work, came from his upbringing. Garrett maintains a high level of expectations at work. This link connects his upbringing, current family, and the children he works with.

Support while growing up came from his mom's relatives; very little contact came from his dad's side after the split-up. His mom was a single mom, and that is a challenge by itself; couple that with raising several children, all close in age. Once his parents divorced, the children saw little of their dad. He moved several hundred miles away, too far to participate in typical day-to-day activities of young school-aged children.

Garrett's mom worked hard to keep her family together. She taught Garrett and his siblings to conquer their daily problems. They arrived home from school before she returned home from work, and while they did not like this routine, they learned to cope with it. Mom made it clear that she loved them; this was visible to the children even when she worked extra hours. His mom's work helped Garrett appreciate the depth of her love for her children. Mom was always generous with her time and effort toward the family. He grew concerned about her at times, but even if she did overdo it, Garrett knew that her resourcefulness made all the difference. She succeeded with her goal of keeping the family together.

Going to church was mandatory; religion was one of the important parts of family life. Through church, they learned the basics of respect, caring for others, not hurting others, and not lying. These and other teachings proved useful later in Garrett's life. Hypocrisy was the word Garrett used when his parents did not attend church and pushed the children to go, but his grandparents did attend with them, as they were active church members themselves. After Garrett's dad left, they continued to attend services. Garrett's mom got the children ready to go, and his grandparents attended with them.

Garrett's grandfather brought the family to an African-American church, which maintained a connection with two standard Protestant churches in the country. Garrett's grandparents taught him and his siblings about traditions, including honor thy mother, honor thy father, and many other aspects of today's normal church life. Incorporating these values into daily life, not just on Sunday mornings, was the standard Garrett's parents and grandparents set for their children.

It was easy to get in trouble if Garrett and his siblings did not live up to the adults' expectations. The family maintained a strong connection with his teacher, who attended the same church and taught Sunday school. In Garrett's life, if something were wrong on a Friday, he would likely hear about it on Sunday. That same routine applied to Sunday and Monday.

Garrett did not like his dad's lack of contact, and he felt resentful at times. Some of his siblings kept in contact with their dad while others kept their distance. Garrett was upset and thought it was his dad's job to be in touch. This remained his attitude even as an adult. When his dad died at a young age, Garrett had some regrets. Besides religious sayings that came to mind about wrath, questions emerged about his dad's interaction with the family after the divorce. It was possible that his dad did the best he could under the circumstances, and perhaps these circumstances were totally unknown to the children.

After his father died, Garrett became more conscious of every minute of his own life. This includes being more aware of everything—from the people important to him, to his work relationships, to how he spends time with family. Garrett's philosophy today reflects an acute awareness of how short life really is and the importance of connection. This affects home life. More time and attention go to family members; trivial things are let go of quickly. Garrett talks with his mom at least weekly and he does home life and work life with a lot of zest. He sees himself as having about the same energy, enthusiasm, and positive focus when he and his son tend the garden as when he attends a work meeting. His family enjoys routine outings, which are often local and do not cost very much. He and his wife want to expose their children to the outdoors and nature as much as possible.

Garrett noted that his mom and grandparents' love for him was one of the underlying factors that made it possible for him to push himself as he did. It was like leaning on a solid rock; their support was unwavering. Another factor that played an important role was the small town where he grew up. It was a comfortable place to live; children were free to play outdoors without parents hovering over them. Small town life sometimes leads to restricted ways of thinking, but in his family's case, community connections far outweighed that concern. Garrett's children have visited his hometown, met relatives, friends, and neighbors, and they sometimes stayed overnight. He and his wife decided that their children should know both sides of their family and its history; they believe family visits are one of the best ways to meet that goal.

∞

Garrett mentioned the importance of his family's devotion to caring for him and his siblings, as well as their teachings about hard work and perseverance. This resulted in lessons in resilience and the inner knowledge that there is a path to overcoming obstacles, no matter what those obstacles are in life.

Stephanie
"Trying Times"

Stephanie's comments about deliberately making her own choices and learning to set firm boundaries reflect resilience developed through inner determination and perseverance. As a hair stylist, Stephanie was creative and enterprising; she was always willing to share clever ideas with others.

When I think of back... [First, I think of childhood and then of marriage.] ... I'm going to go to marriage because of the growth spurt involved... It was a... whirlwind romance. He seemed to be in a good place. [He remained close to his mom though did he not have a solid connection with his dad.] He managed the restaurant he worked at, and he was busy opening other restaurants for the owners.

We got married and then my sister had five strokes. We almost lost her... His mother was diagnosed with cancer... given six months to live. All this stress on my husband caused problems. [After his mom's diagnosis, I found drugs] in the house that I didn't know about, so I [confronted him]. This is not the kind of man I married, and I asked him to decide if he wanted to stick [together] or go an entirely different route.

We made it through a lot. He wasn't... good at family relationships, so I started helping him... We started having relatives over for Thanksgiving dinner, things like that. We had a good marriage at that point. Then, credit problems developed, which we were also able to take care of... I wanted to have a child, but his focus was all over the place. I wanted to get the house together, get the jobs together, and start a family. We got past all these issues and I thought we had a great marriage.

We had one child. We had rough times... I've always been a thin person but... during the pregnancy, I... became bloated with toxemia... I was at high risk; both my son and I were in intensive care at the time of his birth. I had an emergency C-section, it was seventy-two hours since I had any rest, and [my husband] wanted me down there with [our] son. I just couldn't physically do it... I couldn't really help the baby at all for a while... I knew nurses took good care of our son for me, but my husband just didn't get it... This led to the first time I was dependent on him rather than him being dependent on me.

He was supposed to stay there and help me, but he was afraid to take time off work, so he left and went back to work. He worked and I was a stay-at-home mom, but I had socked away enough money so he wouldn't have to worry about anything. In this manner, I was still the caretaker in the relationship... We had two difficult years close to my pregnancy, but I thought maybe we could get back on track. I really wanted the marriage to work and lived in denial during that time.

At the time of our eight-year anniversary, I especially had feelings that something wasn't quite right. He sat me down, said he loved me but wasn't in love with me, and wanted a divorce. The baby was about two years old. I didn't see it coming, his leaving; I just had a bad feeling overall. I ran out of the house and collapsed outside.

I pulled up my bootstraps... went to counseling. I got strength from within myself, but I lost thirty pounds within a few weeks. I was eating; it was just stress... I might have lost it all except for the two-year-old I had in my life. I was determined to become the best possible mom... Regardless of our counselor's view... which was that in spite of it all we should try again, there was no way to do it. He was simply not available even if I would have been. He went to one session and [expressed complaints, but that was it]. There was no winning for us in this situation.

I had a lot of sorting out to do during counseling. I wanted to become a better person. My therapist eventually... [ended routine sessions and declared] that I knew all the right things to do... I refused to look at myself as a victim. I knew I had some of life's challenges. I also knew I had a beautiful son and a husband who apparently could not break out of his old mold... I had to move on. I know I made the right choice. I thought, "How could I become the person and mom I want to be?" I looked at it... as a challenge. Even though it was extremely painful [to face and work through], I knew I was a good person and I would find better things out of [this work]...

Another man came into my life a long time later [that] had also been through a... difficult marriage. We found we had a lot in common and could talk easily. We had similar attitudes in life, in parenting ideas, and in relationships. He was only in town for four months on a business-training trip and I thought, "Great. We can enjoy each other's company and he'll never have to get to know my son." I wanted to keep that space.

However, he became my boyfriend instead. We got together in a way that allowed both of us to grow. He still traveled out of state on a routine basis to see his children who lived with their mother.

I remained skeptical quite a while in the beginning, making sure that this person was the genuine article, that he was who he claimed to be in actions, not just in words and fancy ideas. My son recently revealed he was pleased for me about this relationship. My boyfriend's daughters and I have grown really close as we visit whenever he brings them to this area.

Everything is starting to fall into place, and after all that pain and hard work, I'm starting to reap the benefits of those struggles... It's a struggle for children involved in divorce. [His daughters] want to be with their mom and... they also confided that they wouldn't want to be without me. That's just so precious... His older daughter asked, "How come I'm not like my mom and more like you?" I told her that God put us together so obviously you needed me for something... You know you can come to me and talk about anything—you're a female, I'm a female. That's one thing. We had a good laugh about it. That's a huge metamorphosis.

School is another issue in my own life. My boyfriend helped me out financially. I didn't have a lot of time to do it, so I chose something I could handle on my own. That's how I got into the beauty business. I can make my own hours and that's really helpful. I needed to be a mom and that's the choice I made. My son was complaining about his dad and stepmom the other day. [I explained to] him [that] he has a gift of seeing so much so clearly in his young life... I told him that when he gets caught up in turmoil in life... he has choices to make about things, to look at it as two directions to go in. Then he has to live with the consequences of those choices. He must answer to himself for what he does. That's probably been the one thing that's kept me going. I was determined to make choices and make the choices for myself. I felt that as much as I loved my husband, we were not meant to be together. There was no reason to be mean to him.

My fight was for my son with regard to his dad, but I had to give that up. They do see each other, but maybe not the way my son would have liked. I can't do more and that's another important thing to come to grips with. I get caught in various traps and catch myself and then re-establish and keep my boundaries. Sometimes it takes a few times before boundaries get firmly established. Sometimes it takes longer. It's just important to keep catching yourself and regrouping, starting over, picking up from where you left off...

[Way in the past at home, a lot of] hidden things happened, lots of threats. There was a very high risk for mental and emotional abuse as I look back on it... [My mother was difficult to live with. I never used drugs or got into trouble as she thought I did.] I'm such the good girl that I never touched anything... [I felt pressured to leave home] right after high school graduation. I was seventeen. I worked two jobs. The good news part is that I grew up and did well, even though it was a long story along the way... I became stronger throughout my teen years and eventually found a good path for myself. It took time and a lot of hard work.

My grandmother loved me wholeheartedly. I don't think she necessarily understood exactly what gifts she bestowed on me during all those years. She just did it and it became obvious that she believed in me. She gave me something to hang onto. I like peace of mind. I'm always looking for it and I know that about myself now. I had a grandmother who was golden. My grandmother knew something was up, couldn't get it out of me, and stuck by me. My grandmother was the one person in my life who believed in me, and she empowered me to stand up for myself. She believed in me and in everything I did. My grandmother saved my life.

Stephanie's willingness to set her own boundaries and defend herself at a young age reflects inner resilience. Her grandmother's continued support is another one of the means Stephanie used to find the inner strength to solve problems and make wise decisions.

Norm
"In the Blink of an Eye"

Several events throughout Norm's life led to abrupt and dramatic change. One main turning point was when he received a scholarship for his first year of college. He worked as a principal with younger and older students over many years.

Norm's dad worked as a pharmacist in various hospitals during his years in the military. Before those assignments began, pharmacy training kept him away from home more than was desirable. Norm did not get to know his dad well because of the combination of pharmacy training and years of service. He never even saw his dad again once he left for military duty—his dad died young.

Norm pieced together vague memories of his dad over the years. Their first house was in a small town, which later grew to have over 300,000 people in it. His mother worked hard and kept long hours to keep the family together. The siblings took jobs as soon as they could to help the family. One of Norm's jobs was at a recital hall.

Norm excelled in sports. With no set plans for life after high school, he continued with football. A coach from an out-of-state university watched him play and came up to talk with him after the game. This coach offered him a chance to play football, attend school, and obtain a one-year scholarship; he made this full offer right on the spot. Norm questioned whether his grades were high enough and discovered they were fine. He went off as an out-of-state freshman, stayed one year, and then returned home with no money to his name.

Norm made several comments about school. Soccer was especially fun for him. At over 6 feet tall, he looked a bit unusual for that decade. Miscellaneous jobs seemed special at the time, but later he described them as small and ordinary. They helped him grow and learn about himself. That one football game changed his life forever. It paved the way to college for him. Nothing stopped him from gaining an education once it got started. Even part-time school following that first college year was not a hindrance. It was simply one path on the way to completion.

Norm recalled the story of a teacher in early elementary school, Mrs. Z. She cheered him on as he played soccer, and then one day she disappeared. She abruptly left school and was sent to an internment camp. That event really startled Norm as a youngster, stayed with him for many years, and shaped his attitude. Other things that greatly affected him included his dad's absence, his mom's hard work, his multiple and varied jobs, along with the one football game that proved so helpful and influential toward his future.

Norm's mom died when he was just out of his teens. He felt bad that he never let her know how much she did for him and the family. It was a big undertaking to make sure meals were available every day. Living near a Post Exchange (PX) on a military base helped a lot, and Norm felt he had a stable and secure childhood. His grandparents were the beneficiaries of his dad's insurance policy. It annoyed him that his dad's siblings never came to visit, let alone help his mom and her family.

During late teenage years, Norm moved away from home for good. That first college year involved shared living space with fellow students in an old refurbished community center located just off the main campus. After switching schools, the new job of stocking shelves allowed him flexible hours to attend classes. Norm appreciated the job and the flexibility it offered. He switched campuses again and eventually accumulated all the required credits in time for graduation.

Norm was an adult by the time he learned to make plans for the future. During one college year, he received financial help from a prior teacher; she paid one semester's costs. He inquired by letter sometime later about how he could pay her back. Her response was to find someone in the future who needed help and to help that person. Norm's response was to do this exact type of thing over and again.

The realization that some high school teachers were barely a few years older than Norm really stunned him. A high school reunion was the setting for this revelation. Those teachers earned credentials and started work right away. At the end of one of Norm's grocery store jobs, the boss handed him a gift—money to take with him. Of course, Norm knew that it was the store manager making the gift and not the store itself. This boss was another one who made a huge difference in his life. One thing he did was offer Norm flexible hours at work. This was not the first time a boss had helped him regarding earning college credits. Years later, Norm met this grocery store boss at a church gathering—it was a contact most appreciated. It meant a lot at the time, and a lot even now, in remembering how people reached out and helped him when he was in need.

Following those late teen years when Norm first left home, he lived in many different areas. Those years comprised growing up time. It was right after college that he and his wife married. He completed one semester of graduate school before he joined the service. During his time in the service, his wife taught school. He later finished graduate work and obtained a teaching credential. Next, he ran into a college classmate while job hunting. This friend invited him to check out a program just underway that involved juvenile custody students.

Another moment, another blink, and Norm's life changed forever once again. His administrative credential studies began after a year of teaching in his friend's program. Connections persisted throughout life. A principal became a school superintendent while Norm advanced in his own credentials and eventually became a principal. Program ideas emerged regarding children who needed help for various reasons, as well as for juvenile custody students. Several experimental programs existed at this time; it was a creative moment for Norm and his colleagues. Some of these programs became a solid part of the overall educational system, while others fell by the wayside.

A favorite program dealt with younger and older children who came from a variety of situations. All the participants in this program, parents, teachers, staff, and administration, worked toward the betterment of each child and the whole program. Norm was likely to sit and talk with students on a frequent basis, and he found most of them to be good kids, earnest students, who were interested in advancing their own lives, their family's lives, and the community at large.

Norm's ability to go with the flow, follow head and heart, and make wise decisions are all to his benefit. This reflects a base of resilience within him. He credits his mother with providing a solid family life, and this is one key to fostering resilience throughout life.

Bob
"Abrupt Family Life Changes"

Bob learned about boundary setting as the result of a dreadful family accident. These boundaries helped him choose the issues that needed attention and those that he could let go of altogether, or deal with later. Bob found he had the knack of teaching others how to set their own boundaries. He worked with young children at the time of this story.

Bob started his story from about middle elementary school through high school. He had a large number of family members around, and during the holidays, visits went from one family to another over the course of the day, usually in a particular sequence. There were people around who cared about him, yet at the same time, he found himself the one cousin in the 'in-between' age group. Younger and older cousins did not share his interests. It was time to find some other activity to engage in while visiting or get bored. Once he could drive, that made a lot of difference. He stayed long enough for a nice visit, and having a car made it easy for him to leave at the right moment.

Bob considered his life golden. His parents stayed together, and although one sibling was several years younger, he and his brother were close enough in age to play together. They had a solid home life and plenty of friends. He was healthy, had no broken bones, and no real worries. He sometimes thought about what would happen in life, as if something might even all this out. Things continued in this golden manner for several more years. In his early to mid-twenties, however, things did start to even out.

Bob is a confident and upbeat person with the attitude of

having something to look forward to every day. His extended family is partly to thank for that approach to life, although within five years or so the size of that family dwindled. Serious illness took the lives of two close family members. One grandparent became seriously ill. Two or three years later, the family scheduled a trip to celebrate his dad's birthday. On that trip, a car accident took several lives of close relatives, including Bob's dad and a family friend.

His mom was lucky to survive this accident. The head-on collision crushed the car, though later Bob wondered if some members of the family might have survived with seat belts fastened. He planned a social visit with a friend the following day, but once the phone call came, the two of them went directly to the hospital. His mom had surgery and, due to medication, was foggy for a while. She told Bob she sensed death and did not know where everyone was. The official word had not reached them.

It took Bob some time to coordinate with his sister and brother. Other family members were located at different hospitals, so it took even more time to learn what had actually happened. One of Bob's aunts received a call looking for next-of-kin, so she immediately knew something dreadful had occurred. Bob and his siblings formally identified bodies over the next few hours.

He walked around in a bit of a daze and knew it was time to set up funerals. Once he sat down at a mortuary and began talking with someone about specifics, Bob started to feel relieved and more clear-headed. The next challenge proved even more difficult. Back at the hotel, Bob met up with what seemed like a slew of family members who had just arrived for the party, and they asked Bob where everyone was. They hadn't heard about the accident.

Once over the initial shock, Bob received plenty of family support. No one blamed him or his siblings for not being at the right place at the right time or for not taking over driving responsibilities in the first place. They helped as best they could.

No problems occurred with the driver of the other car, which was another relief for Bob. Bob's family had to research financial issues regarding his dad's death. At the same time, they attended funerals, visits, and started to cope with a smaller family size.

The extended visit of his grandmother really helped. Later, his grandmother moved to be nearer her siblings, and she lived there a few months until her death. The family's deaths were shocking for Bob and left him in denial. When his grandma died, it was just too much. That death made him angry. Not only did he miss her, but also enough time had elapsed since the car accident that more of his feelings surfaced. This provided an emotional release. He and his dad were close—they attended local sports games, played the same musical instrument, and became a bit like friends. Whenever Bob invited his dad to watch a game, off they went. Bob was in his mid-twenties when his dad died.

That 'last straw' happened with the death of Bob's grandma. He felt repeatedly kicked around. First, all those family members died at once. Then, his grandma died. This triggered feelings about his mom. First, her husband and sister died. Next, it was her mother, and this was an unexpected death. Some sort of episode occurred, and doctors thought Bob's grandma would make a full recovery. A week later, she died. Bob's mom was okay with this abrupt death, but it was difficult.

Bob underwent some outlook changes throughout these events. When someone mentions they are under stress about such and such, he wonders why they let such trivia bother them. It is often just not worth it. A much worse thing, maybe a full one hundred percent or even worse, could show up tomorrow in your life. Circumstances make it a choice about ever saying this aloud. Bob has learned the art of compartmentalizing, i.e., how to set concerns deliberately aside for a time. This allows Bob to continue with immediate happenings in life. When that big accident happened, there was a shutdown, but it was not a conscious choice at the time. He has since learned how to make conscious choices to set things aside as needed.

Bob went on to acknowledge how compartmentalization has proven useful. When a difficulty arises, for example, and the circumstances are out of his control, he tells himself not to stress over it. Instead, his goal is to carry on with an alternate task, one that is in his realm to accomplish. Sometimes there is nothing in his power to do about a given situation. In that case, it is best to shut down worry before it starts. Why add stress when it could not help? Earlier in life, Bob tended to look for a quick resolution, especially in work situations, regardless of his place in whatever was going on. He deliberately chooses how to spend work energy now. That is, he makes firm and conscious decisions and then goes for it.

Bob knew that he had an upbeat attitude regardless of life's difficulties. Even though his large family was gone, there were things that he was happy about and grateful for. A large family might come back to him in a different way. Sometime later, his role might switch from son to dad in family life, and that offers a nice image. Fishing is an activity Bob enjoys with a friend and his friend's dad. Other things his friend and his dad do together as son and dad give Bob a good feeling. They provide a pleasant reminder of the things he and his dad enjoyed together.

Bob fostered a positive attitude with the students he worked with. One goal was to plant seeds of success. His influence went in the direction of getting through any difficulty, coming out the other side, and recognizing strength through it all. Bob's hope was that they would look back one day and remember something he communicated with them that led them to make good decisions.

∞

Bob's gratefulness and acknowledgment about a strong family life reflect resilience. The family accident was one of those events where Bob demonstrated an ability to make something good out of something bad, which is another factor of resilience. He used this skill, as well as boundary setting, in his work with children.

Nadia
"Visits with Dad"

Nadia and I attended graduate school, worked on projects, and studied together.

Nadia's dad lived with a serious disease for around twenty years when she shared this story. Her mom was his main caregiver, and for most of those years, she managed their house, garden, and landscaping. Her mom was also the primary person who kept her dad as physically active as he was during those years. Once her parents moved to be near Nadia, things changed—they probably had been changing all along.

Nadia's dad eventually had to move to a small group home and later to a nursing home as his condition worsened. He could no longer manage well enough on his own. Nadia's mom could not get him from one room to another with just a nudge on that walker any longer. No matter what, his decline continued. His personal efforts were enormous; he worked as hard as he could have.

Nadia took her parents on outings that benefited all of them. One location was a drive along a country road to a lake. Another was to a favorite family restaurant where her dad felt comfortable and welcomed by the owner. In their new location, Nadia took on the task of getting them to doctor's offices and taking care of other errands. Her parents lived close enough to walk to a grocery store when they were up to it. Both parents used walking as a form of exercise on a routine basis when it was possible.

Early one morning, about half-awake, Nadia had an image of her grandparents. They were cheerfully waving to her, though they let her know they came to see her dad, their son-in-law—Nadia needed to step aside. At the same time, Nadia noticed an image of her dad, fragile, hesitant. She shared this dream with her dad; he had not thought about any of them recently. They talked about her dad's brother who had died of cancer during the past year. In her dad's mind's eye, his bother looked just great and smiled a lot. He thought of his brother frequently. She and her dad spoke together about these family members; they were glad and even relieved to have positive images of them.

Nadia mentioned the black bread her grandfather used to share with them on Sunday afternoon visits; her dad's eyes lit up. It was time to put this idea together! Her dad agreed. Soon after, Nadia and her dad enjoyed that treat from long ago. It even included whiskey and ginger ale, just a few sips; this was her dad's old-time favorite.

Nadia asked her dad what he was thinking about; he wanted to be prepared to say hello. When asked if he was talking about grandparents, his response was "Yes, it was an omen." The two of them commiserated when he asked again how to get prepared. Grandpa on her mom's side went around saying good-bye to neighbors the day before he died. Did Dad think Grandpa decided it was time—when Dad said yes, this was another omen.

Nadia's dad then asked if she had any sharp objects with her and told her he was looking for one. She did not and when she asked what it was for, he could not say. Nadia asked about how the illness had worn him down and limited his movements. She wondered if this had anything to do with his asking for sharp instruments. Nadia felt bad about not being able to help her dad. They talked a little more but to the real satisfaction of neither of them.

Her dad asked her about what a person does when their back is against the wall. She tried to answer but did not know how. When she asked him if his back was against the wall, he said yes. He got teary and they hugged during this emotional moment. It did not solve his determination that his life was over beyond this simple recognition, although the talk had value for both of them.

Nostalgic visits occurred as well. They discussed fun memories, such as the fishing trips of Nadia's childhood. As a youngster, her dad encouraged her to stick up for herself and for her own ideas. There was no need to listen to others when she knew she was right. They had a huge giggle about a catfish and an eel Nadia caught one summer. She held her dad's hand and he held hers tightly. They ended the visit with his request for blue cheese to go with that black bread during the next visit. This treat had become a much-appreciated routine for both of them.

Nadia found the angler's calendar she was looking for. On the next visit, they looked at calendar pictures and decided on a place to hang them. His favorite pictures are now on his door at a height most beneficial for his viewing pleasure. Before she hung them up, he got to see each picture close up. Nadia's dad got teary again and told her he worried about her. She reassured him as best she could that she and the family supported him one hundred percent and were on his side regarding his life.

They talked about additional fishing and boating trips during another visit. Nadia's dad told her he enjoyed seeing the pictures so much and they made him happy. Her youngest brother was about to arrive for a visit, and Nadia's dad asked her to pick up a special bottle of wine for the occasion. It pleased him when she showed up with it.

There were some conferences coming up in Nadia's schedule. She was to make two presentations over a brief period. She was nervous; her dad reassured her that she would do just fine. After the first two minutes, she would sail through the talks. She appreciated his reassurance and support. These talks provided a different avenue of discussion for both of them, and they gave Nadia's dad one more reason to smile. His approach throughout life was to contribute, problem solve, and find other options in tough situations.

It was such a dilemma about the request for a sharp object. Today, it appears more options exist regarding end of life issues. A cancer patient Nadia heard about recently chose to stop chemo. That patient's life continued until it ended, naturally, according to the patient's wishes. It is possible to fill out papers, which direct the desired treatment or lack of it, for use when a person reaches the stage of 'no hope for recovery.' Nadia's brother was correct in his comment that tube feeding became an 'extreme measure' once their dad reached a certain stage in his day-to-day physical condition. Their dad's goal, and part of his stated wishes, was to live life with dignity and find dignity at the time of death.

Nadia took the opportunity of telling this story to encourage people to gain knowledge, investigate options on their own behalf, and to help loved ones investigate options on matters involving living and dying with dignity.

Clyde
"Keep Moving and Stay Busy"

Clyde worked with younger students at the time of this talk. He often participated in after-school activities and went on field trips with them.

Clyde started his story as a preschool or kindergarten age child. He and his brother did not have many neighborhood friends their own age, so they mainly played together. As best friends, they had matching clothes and matching bikes for several years. They grew close and remained so over the years. His brother was quite a bit different from Clyde—he was a true adventurer and a strong leader. It was good for Clyde to watch his older brother, the enterprising one; sometimes he followed his brother's lead.

His brother influenced him to try many activities that Clyde would never touch otherwise. Clyde felt confident he would survive some random activity if his brother survived it first. As the far more adventurous one, Clyde's brother was also the first to get in trouble. Clyde's choice became the activity his brother accomplished without getting into any kind of trouble. This brother had a tremendous influence and overall impact on Clyde's life.

Their dad had some problems that kept him increasingly away from the family. Clyde's older brother and their dad had similar personality styles, and instead of connecting, this contributed to them getting in each other's way and into disagreements. His brother was outright, expressive and a strong thinker, as was his dad. Clyde was quiet and did not make a fuss; sometimes he did what he wanted in a way that brought no notice to him.

One night, Clyde had a nightmare and went to his parents'

bedroom for a hug—he hoped to sleep with them. This scenario repeated itself several times that night and his dad sent him back to bed each time. This final time, Clyde's dad actually carried him back and let him drop abruptly onto the mattress. No one was hurt but when their grandparents heard that story later, they grew concerned. Clyde did not say much, but his brother told them that their dad should have been more careful, that he actually scared both of them. Clyde acknowledged that his brother watched out for him that time and he still does. They live close by and engage in many activities together. Clyde retains a lot of respect and admiration for his brother.

Dad was a little scary at other times too. He was aloof, strict, and verbally loud. Eventually, he left the family; at some point later, Clyde's parents divorced. Clyde has not engaged much with him since then. If his dad were not interested, then Clyde would not spend energy in that direction.

When Clyde thinks about his life, people come up as number one in importance, especially those who have influenced him in positive ways. His siblings play an important role for him; he described his mom as way beyond outstanding and awe-inspiring. Both living with his dad and his dad's separation from the family are two examples of what Clyde took time to deal with. Other family members are a positive influence, fun to be around, and fun to visit whenever possible.

Clyde added comments about his dad's influence and the year he was able to spend on a college campus. He learned a lot about how to bounce back, start over, and move forward in his life, especially when his dad first left the family. This change in family life helped Clyde develop a wider perspective on issues and gain a broader picture of possibilities. Although he treasures his year of college on campus and away from home, coupling that year with a return to a different school, and employment the following year, prepared Clyde for living life well.

Many things have a way of working out; although it was not an easy experience when he first returned home, Clyde developed workable ideas in this situation. He wrote up a list of possible jobs to apply for after his return. Psychology was a strong interest since early elementary school—he wanted to learn more about what makes people tick.

Clyde liked to keep busy, to have something to do, somewhere to go, and some action to take. Once home, he restarted music lessons, participated in a church program, renewed his own spirituality, and got involved in hiking and other physical challenges. His favorite is hiking; the more difficult the hike, the better he likes it. The absorption is calming and restorative. Getting out into the countryside both relaxes and challenges him depending on the difficulty level chosen for that day. These outdoor activities require concentration, which keeps Clyde focused. There is no room for worries about other issues. He finds this therapeutic as well as enjoyable.

His actions say a lot for him because as an introvert, he does not talk all that much even now. It was more so that way for him in elementary school. Sometimes, as a youngster, his brother helped convey to their parents what Clyde wanted to say. To balance this quietness, and to gain recognition and a sense of achievement, Clyde learned to push himself toward excellence in other ways at an early age. He learned fancy bike tricks, dramatic skating moves with friends, and he worked hard for high grades in school. This translated easily into physical and other challenges that Clyde gives himself today as a young adult.

∞

Clyde continued by reiterating the things he sees as useful for a healthy lifestyle. This includes family, friends, and a renewed spiritual life. It continues with deliberate decisions and chosen activities. Education, music, and physical activity play a part in his life. When he learned how to overcome a challenge in those areas, it enhanced his confidence in overcoming obstacles in other parts of life. Even small accomplishments helped relieve anxiety and tension; Clyde's examples included pulling weeds and washing dishes.

Matt
"Barely in the Nick of Time"

Matt's biggest lesson was in setting a boundary for home life that copied what was successful at work and living up to it. He worked with teenagers on structuring their own lives for success. This story explains how he taught his daughter some of those same lessons.

Matt's life at work went smoothly most days. Home life became increasingly difficult as his teenager grew older and challenged him more often. He needed to chart a different course. His softhearted approach was no longer useful, and his wife let him know it. It often does not work for only one parent to be the disciplinarian, and it is worse if the two parenting styles differ sharply. Matt consulted with colleagues and friends. It finally dawned on him that the structure of his workday, teaching teenagers how to cope and become successful out in the world, might work for him at home with the proper setup. The family had to redefine itself and find a bottom line all members could live by. It is far better for a family to initiate structure when children are young. An example Matt gave was teaching toddlers about chores—to put those large Legos they play with back in the toy box. He and his wife devised a contract the two of them and their daughter could use successfully.

The beauty of setting a contract is that once it is set, you, the parent, simply use it. It is okay to rely on it. With their teenager, phone privileges and visits with friends counted for a lot. They set up a plan that no longer tolerated screaming, yelling, and in particular cursing, especially toward Mom [the original family disciplinarian]. Tying together privileges with grades in school, behaviors, and chores helped Matt and his wife diffuse situations rather than escalate them. Both parents' participation to the fullest helped their daughter grow with the program.

Carrying on and whining by the child or teenager does not cut it. Playing one parent against the other no longer works. These behaviors are simply not part of the program and come with consequences. Parents must communicate the consequences to their children ahead of time so they will understand what will happen if they choose to misbehave. Detail is more important if the child is older when the program starts.

Matt shared examples of how this worked. When his daughter used rude language, her mom learned to respond with a two-word consequence—for example, 'no phone' or 'no friends.' That meant no calls or visits the rest of that day. It also meant no discussion about consequences. Their daughter complained to her dad at first about her mom not being fair about it. Then she complained to him that she did not mean to say it, it slipped out by total accident, could she take it back, could she still at least make one call? He relied on the contract. Bad language equals no calls and no visits. Period. Amen. No discussion. Tomorrow is another day; every day offered a fresh start. That fresh start is an enormously important part of the contract. Hidden resentments hinder rather than help these situations.

During junior high, neither his daughter nor her friends were the studious type, and she earned mostly "C" grades. Once in high school, though, her school changed, friends changed, and grades improved. She now usually earned "B" or higher grades. Her current friends, a mixture of mainly Hispanic and Caucasian, are very academically oriented. College is on their minds. His daughter has no interest in boyfriends, although she maintains friendships with both boys and girls. Matt expressed a great deal of relief at this switch in attitude on his daughter's part and thinks that the home contract contributed to the change. He believes several other factors played a role. These include one teacher's influence, maturity gained over high school years, and the whole college application process, which is now a daily conversation topic.

Matt's daughter loves to drive. He and his wife agreed that this privilege, connected to the right behavior, is a powerful reinforcement. They clarified the idea that what means something to their daughter is what counts and what will work. What they each see as reinforcement does not matter much. Because of a personal interest in this driving privilege, their daughter has taken steps necessary to maintain it. Matt and his wife have adjusted this home program according to their daughter's maturity level over the years; new contracts occur as things change. He again mentioned that it is best to start this type of program much earlier in a child's life; their daughter was almost twelve when they started their program. Once their daughter starts college, they will split the cost of a used car with her. A new car after graduation, with a job in hand, will become solely her responsibility.

Their daughter had one experience with too much alcohol. She got sick right in the middle of a party at a friend's house; that was her one and only binge drinking session, and it was enough to last a lifetime. She went on to tell her parents it was a strong lesson, and other than the room spinning and racing to the restroom, nothing else bad happened. Matt and his wife have confidence about their daughter's commitment to avoiding drugs. Drugs are easily obtainable through high school contacts; however, she and her friends have made it clear that they will not go that way.

As a family, they are looking into scholarships along with college application forms. Matt expects his daughter to attend a state university, which is more affordable for them as a family. He hopes she will go to a four-year school right from the start, but he is waiting to see what develops.

Once Matt brought home the needed structure, family life improved and his daughter learned many useful life lessons. This approach helped Matt teach his daughter about self-discipline, making wise decisions, and solving problems. His daughter used these skills to build success in her later career in medicine.

Aliza
"A New Beginning"

A major turning point in Aliza's life was in a move to the United States. She was the owner of a successful local restaurant at the time of this interview, and she maintained strong connections with regular customers.

Aliza reflected that divorce makes so many changes in one's life, not just in the primary relationship. Sometimes people find themselves more dependent on others, or on the other hand, it makes them more demanding of others. In some parts of the world, for example in the Middle East, moving freely is unusual, especially for a female. Divorce is not all right in many places; it is not okay when no husband is in sight. In some countries, once the child reaches a certain age, fathers get first choice regarding custody.

Aliza's family continued to support her throughout the divorce and wearying custody issues. She defended her position and ideas about custody, which made it harder to get through the legal arena. Some ideas were not against the law itself, but they were not all right for women to have a voice about. Mom is supposed to remain quiet and just go along with things. Regarding custody issues, a dad does not pursue custody for his daughters the way he often does for his son. Part of the culture's emphasis is on women living up to the expectations of others. It took time to sort out custody issues, but eventually it did work out.

Her family continued with support and care for her son. When first in the States, she was here alone. She had the push and stamina necessary for success, although she knew it would be difficult in getting started. Aliza was thrilled to know that living here, she was equal to others; it did not matter how much money she had. She was free to move forward, to take initiative.

Aliza commented that in the States, following the law counts more than background. Life here is nothing like the man's world of her home country. Here, she could report harassment and get assistance. It does not work that way back home. Harassment against women typically goes unpunished; complaints pile up on the desk and are ignored or thrown out. The law is not protective across the board.

Aliza earned university level training in economics back home.

Once she arrived here, she worked at a few jobs to get her feet on the ground, eventually making her way into the business world, and she now runs a successful entrepreneurial enterprise.

She was able to raise her son, who is now a successful professional working in computers and electronics. Aliza said that as much as humans take pride in and want to raise their children at home, it is important to remember that they need to become independent young adults. They must get out on their own, learn to spread their own wings, and learn to fend for themselves.

Aliza had work experience in the family's business back home. The family helped her get started here in various ways. Her siblings gave guidance in the move and business idea development. Aliza's capability and drive gave her the confidence to move ahead with business plans once she felt settled enough.

Aliza loves this area and the people she works with. It is especially thrilling to get to know her customers, and it feels like being an integral part of the community due to owning a restaurant. Aliza's coworkers tease her and suggest going out more, even on a date, but she is happy to stay at work. The conversations back and forth with her regular customers are enjoyable and include getting to know them and learning about their families. While employed back home, she spent quite a bit of time in Europe on business ventures for one large company. In addition to travel time, it also meant a lot of business hustle and bustle. She really appreciates this change in life to something simpler and quieter.

The undertaking of coming here was scary and thrilling. All siblings lived elsewhere, so she was fully on her own in the beginning. It was quite a challenge to arrive as an individual alone and find that first job here. At the same time, it was the best move ever; it helped both mentally and emotionally. She witnessed her strength in action in a new country.

Aliza credits her parents for bringing their children up with an independent streak. Her parents took their own education seriously and made good use of it through their work years. They taught Aliza that education and work contribute to a healthy way of living. This is a different approach from other families with different backgrounds back home, where girls are much more restricted through their growing up years and after. Aliza and her siblings were not restricted but encouraged to venture out and find their own paths in life.

Aliza's parents lived in the States at the time of this story. They help each other out, both at home and at the restaurant. A loving, caring family is how Aliza describes them; she is grateful they are here now. It is a wonderful contrast to being here alone and just getting started. There were plenty of questionable moments in those early days. Strong and okay is how her son describes Aliza now.

A peaceful outlook, daily enjoyment, and appreciation are part of Aliza's current life. She is grateful about many things and believes that being fully alive today can happen right along with preparing for tomorrow. She shared a few philosophical thoughts. With some effort, people can live in a peaceful manner every day, and trust would increase if people felt confident about themselves and their lives. Lowering one's stress level would help; the next part is the individual's decision to move ahead in one's life. Maintaining a positive approach to life, even without being religious, is what Aliza learned as a child.

Counting blessings, getting an education, setting priorities and goals, and making concrete accomplishments are among the things Aliza's family stressed. They also taught their children that the way to avoid misunderstandings is to learn to be clear in the first place. Personal inner strength is the best way to face difficulties, and true recovery comes from deep inside a person. Even though people have talks with their minister, etc., it is more important to stand up and think for him or herself. Education is the basic right of everyone and it is a fundamental aspect of a healthy life.

Aliza remained grateful for her life's foundation; her goal is to keep going forward and to keep growing. A positive attitude contributes to life's success, and she influences others through an optimistic approach. Starting with a strong family life, Aliza's story provides a shining example of resilience.

Shari
"On My Own Terms at Last"

Shari has worked successfully in private practice as a marriage and family counselor for many years.

Shari went through a lot of distress as a youngster; she felt little kindness at home. Turmoil was the norm. This came from her mom's stress responses. Her dad helped a lot by his gentle mannerisms, but he could not see to every issue. She knew her mom would get upset, and that could happen at any moment. There was a daily question about what was going to happen in the next minute or in the next ten minutes. Shari's daily life became kind of like walking on a tightrope.

Comfort and warm fuzzy feelings of childhood came mainly from Shari's dad. He commiserated at times about distressful happenings going on in their home. He also participated in normal parenting behaviors on a routine basis. This included checking schoolwork and teachers' notes, fixing regular meals, listening to book reports, and listening to his children's fun stories. He did all this to the best of his ability, and he exerted effort with endless patience and support for the children. He really wanted his children to have a solid education and a strong foundation for their futures.

Shari's mom seemed to participate mainly in response to something that went wrong. Name-calling was involved, which Shari especially disliked. She was grateful to get out of the house; sometimes this happened when she helped her dad with his house calls as a pediatrician. At times, she waited in the car; other times, she went inside with him. Watching him at work fascinated her.

During high school, she sometimes worked in her dad's office as an extra helper. She learned a lot from watching him. His caring, listening, and suggestions to help a family through difficult times rubbed off. She chose a different field, but it is definitely a field where she could help others.

In Shari's own mind, her mom had quite a few diagnoses. She simply would not go along with her mother's comments and requests, and she rebelled instead of complying. Household chores were not enjoyable, and she became especially annoyed when her mother instructed Shari and her sisters to complete various chores while it looked like their mom just sat around. In later years, their mother mellowed a bit, time alone may have helped. An additional possibly is that two of her daughters went into the psychology field while the other daughter attended frequent therapy sessions over a few years.

One of Shari's sisters attempted to placate, or take care of, her mother in some ways. Their mom was not in a position to tolerate frustration. Sometimes the siblings, although they knew they had plenty of food and clothes, wanted more. They wanted some active encouragement, and their mom was not up to it.

Shari reasoned that because her mother was upset whether she performed the requested task or not, she might as well not do that task. Doing it seemed like an extra energy drain. One time when Shari quoted from a book about how to speak to children, her mother countered by saying that it was obvious that the author did not know anything about raising children.

Even casual shopping with her mother could be troublesome. When things became loud, Shari would walk away to a different part of the store for a while. She pretended to be shopping alone until things settled down. Shari's mother got upset one day after an elementary school friend went home. Her mother thought the girl would complain that their house was not clean enough. Nonetheless and even with alternate options offered and paid for, Shari's mother refused to hire a housekeeper.

When Shari was older and moved into her own home, she did hire a housekeeper. Something about the earlier repeated scene of housework, mother yelling, the idea that it was never good enough, did not sit well and Shari found a way around it. This proved immensely helpful in adult life, especially once she had her own family.

Professionally, Shari's mother went into the medical field. During training, her mother saw herself as the person on the other end of the phone—the one obviously upset about a million things. This bothered her mother quite a bit, yet Shari wondered how and even if, a connection might develop. She knew that her mother had troubles during her own upbringing and thought she might have low self-esteem.

Shari eventually received education and training in psychology and works as a therapist. She credited that choice to her mother's influence, especially because of the early years of upheaval in the family household. Shari's mother received advanced training and continued to work in the medical field. Shari used humor in her own life and gained a lot from her work as client and therapist.

Resilience developed early. Challenges to her mom's actions reflect a deep-seated belief that Shari herself was okay, but something was wrong in the household. Shari's ability to cope with later challenges connects to the development of strong boundaries and inner confidence.

SIX

Parker
"Never Give Up"

A key turning point occurred when Parker suddenly had the opportunity to attend graduate school, which allowed her to take a long-term dream and build it into a reality. Parker worked as a librarian in a variety of locations and dealt with younger and older children. Her words encouraged everyone she met.

Parker was one of those folks who knew exactly what she wanted to do in early elementary school. She wanted to be a librarian. As a young student, she read better than fellow students did, and her teacher asked her to help the class put a play together. Scholastic books were available and she put sign-out slips in them and distributed them around the class. This became direct practice for her future career.

Parker thought that life would go according to her early plan—school, college, and library work. There were many surprises along the way, and some were not to her liking. She expected, as part of college or library work, that she would meet someone and then he and she would marry. It did not work out that way. There were many difficulties before the opportunity for library school opened up. Parker wound up cramming in more classes than her peers had to because of time constraints. As she thought over earlier plans, she wondered why she faced so many challenges along the way.

A master's degree is required for librarian training. Parker worked full time for a private company and went to school part time, usually at night. She had to alternate semesters between school and work in order to afford school during most of that time. Parker also had to take out a bank loan to continue her studies. At one point, the school gave her a scholarship to cover the cost of one final class. Parker volunteered at a rescue mission during graduate training days, and she did so typically on weekends. She became involved with children in attendance, and she brought in a variety of arts and crafts projects to work on. Parker was pleased to see the same children return weekend after weekend. She enjoyed getting to know them.

Some fellow classmates sailed through graduate school in less than two years, while it took her five. That is the way life was for her. She had to work her way through, and she continued the best she could regardless of the time involved or how difficult it really was at times. Nothing stopped her. Once she finished school, it was time to look for actual librarian work. This meant saying good-bye to mission work, which provided one of her life's treasures. Parker found a job at a school dealing with both younger and older children. It was exactly the right moment; the room was workable, the books to start with were waiting for her, and her new colleagues offered to help her set things up. Everyone was ready to go, including the students.

Parker shared these comments. People should learn what their strengths and interests are. They should set a goal for themselves and make a plan to reach it. Sometimes obstacles might hinder that plan; changes may be required or an alternate route might have to be developed. People have to learn to stick up for themselves and ignore others sometimes. Their approach may be different, or take longer, but it is still theirs.

Parker's determination at a young age provided a model for her later pursuits. She kept plans going and she overcame obstacle after obstacle along the way. This shows an unwavering attitude toward accomplishment that demonstrates resilience.

Madalyn
"My Brother on Angels' Wings"

As a young person, Madalyn worked with younger children. She engaged them with stories and asked questions that helped the children learn to think.

Madalyn was working with younger children when she learned of the passing of a colleague's mother. Another colleague brought in a card for everyone to sign. She wondered about how tough this must be for him. This man was close with both his parents, and as this death was unexpected, it would likely be difficult to cope with. In theory, Madalyn compared this loss with the loss of someone who had been ill a long time, or with someone who lived to be over one hundred years old. She wondered about the impact of each type of death and prayed for this colleague.

Less than a week later, she was busily working with the younger children on an enjoyable crafts project. One brother, the comedian of the family, called. She asked him what was going on, because it was unusual for the family to call at work. He requested that she come right home. She explained that she was busy working with youngsters and was in the middle of a messy project, but he insisted. Madalyn's brother delayed in answering further questions. When she confronted him about it, he mentioned only that an accident had happened. Madalyn asked for details, but her brother repeated his request for her to come right home and told her he could tell her better there. This was the first she knew that something had happened to one of their brothers, that there had been an accident.

Madalyn decided to go home but first gratefully distracted herself by talking with the children and cleaning up the art project. The children helped as much as they could and expressed their concern about her. Other staff members tried to usher her out quickly, but it did not work. She thought the delay would make things better at home.

She made a phone call to a friend on the way home and asked for prayers. Madalyn shared that something weird happened in her family; she mentioned that one of her brothers might have died. The friend listened and responded in a caring and supportive way.

Next, Madalyn called a male friend who was close over a number of years. Something was up, and they agreed to meet right away. He offered to pick her up, but she told him to wait at his house, that she would be right there. He lived close to her parents' house, and Madalyn wanted to have her car nearby to use later. This friend was a close enough friend to the whole family, so he found out the news just before she arrived. He cried as he told Madalyn that her brother died that morning. A flash, quicker than lightning, went through her head. It was about the brother she pictured earlier that day. He flew a small plane and it crashed that morning. There were no survivors. In a split second, her life changed forever.

Her worst-case scenario had just come true. Everything was different now. Madalyn started thinking a million things at once; she was concerned for everyone involved. This included her parents, his fiancée, other family members, and her brother's friends. How could she be there; what would help anyone? Sobbing, she sat with her friend and then told him it was time to get home. She needed to figure out how to support her family, be there for her parents, and support her brother's fiancée.

Her friend drove her to the family's home and suddenly everything seemed different. Madalyn was used to happy activity with youngsters visiting grandparents, siblings chatting, and in-laws talking with each other. Although the family had grown in the years since her brother's death, the style of visits largely remained constant. It was not that way this time. There were lots of tears and hugs; family members supported each other. She hugged everyone in turn and felt a need to be strong for others.

Madalyn had no idea what to say, or what would help. She realized that everyone's loss was different—son, brother, nephew, grandson. In her mind's eye, her brother sat among angels in heavenly skies. That idea helped her internally, but she chose not to talk about it because of the overall sadness she sensed in the house. Madalyn went around to everyone and shared hugs, tears, and conversation; she found that the pain of this young death brought everyone together, even though each person felt that pain differently.

Madalyn made her way to the second floor of the house where her brother's fiancée sat with friends. They were not talking, not crying; they were just there. Emotion was on hold for the moment.

It became obvious to Madalyn that everything was upside down for her brother's fiancée. Wedding music became funeral music. Groomsmen became pallbearers. A beautiful song chosen for the wedding provided a funeral song and theme.

Madalyn appreciated that this group of family and friends were able to stick together and support each other through all this. Once again, she had a keen appreciation for the different experiences of pain various people go through, especially her mother and her brother's fiancée. Madalyn knew part of her role in all this was to provide extra support whenever and wherever possible. When someone offers support, say a shoulder or a listening ear for example, it helps that person almost as much as it helps the person who needs support at the time.

Madalyn's references to a sound family life and to a couple of close, supportive friends illustrate a strong foundation for resilience. Gratefulness about many parts of life, large and small, provides another aspect of that foundation.

Michaela
"Life's Twists and Turns"

Michaela worked many years as a high school science teacher. In that capacity, she often helped teachers of younger students. She did this by setting up displays and organizing materials for many hands-on experiments.

Michaela raised her children on a ranch out in the country. They rode horses and did basic farm chores as a family. They were able to travel and introduce their children to snorkeling and scuba diving when they were old enough. Her husband remained with Michaela until close to the time they started having trouble with their daughters. The trouble happened rather abruptly. Michaela came from a family where everyone got along and followed the rules. It stung when her younger daughter started acting out, didn't get along with teachers, and threatened to run away from home. Drugs remained a high risk for a time.

Several difficult years followed. Her daughter's grades slipped, a teen pregnancy occurred, and a huge car accident soon followed. The car accident, as difficult as it was to get through, woke her daughter up in some ways. She wanted to graduate high school, cleaned up her act quite a bit, and asked for her mom's help in raising the baby so she could break up with the dad, whose lifestyle was too risky. Michaela helped as much as possible, and she was pleased to see her daughter step up and start to move forward. Years later, her daughter was healthy enough to leave a low-keyed job; she was accepted as a recruit for police department training, passed with flying colors, and now works as a full-fledged police detective.

Michaela's older daughter was in many ways the opposite of her younger sister. She was an "A" student across the board, had success in college, and then went for further study abroad. This older daughter made out really well and aced just about every course she took, including graduate work. Then one day she started acting erratically, made frantic calls to a boyfriend back home, and her behavior raised concerns among everyone who knew her at work.

These coworkers contacted her younger sister first, and then they were able to reach Michaela. Even though this older daughter was over twenty-one, and could travel independently, coworkers and friends felt strongly that something was wrong. It looked serious enough that they wanted to make sure that if one of them could accompany this daughter back home, there would be someone available to watch out for her and see to her medical care and recovery needs.

It took a lot to determine what had actually happened. It seemed like a mental or emotional concern, a physical thing going wrong in the brain, or perhaps a neurological issue. This would take a long time for the family, doctors, and various medical clinics to sort through. Once this daughter returned home safe and sound, she calmed down and her recovery looked brighter. Her steadiest boyfriend continued to come around, which provided additional relief for Michaela and her younger daughter.

Eventually, Michaela's older daughter recovered enough to carry on in a normal way. Her high intelligence and emotional stamina helped a lot in this recovery. She was not able to return to work, married that particular boyfriend, and now has a successful marriage and family life.

Michaela said that life was so crammed full of things to do, meetings to attend, doctors and insurance office calls to make, questions to clear up and to answer that she had no time or energy left to process anything. There was no time to feel anything but exhaustion. Michaela had some stomach problems and weight loss due to high stress levels. She worked full time over many years, and she found the ability to separate workday requirements from the rest of life. Michaela carried on in a highly competent fashion in the classroom, listened to and answered students' questions, gave tests, and demonstrated science fundamentals.

Michaela found that letting things sit for a while, carrying on in other aspects of life, such as work or even grocery shopping, then coming back later to unanswered questions and quandaries works well for her. She tends to mull things over a lot and that technique helped in the situations with each of her daughters. Time alone was a huge help. Walking through her yard, gardening, and not having a doctor or a therapist to have to talk with, these simple things helped Michaela's healing process along.

One day while she was walking alone, out in the garden, the tears began to flow, which brought much needed relief. Within a short time, her younger daughter showed up and became concerned, lest she be the reason for the tears. Michaela explained that it was 'all of the above,' which included this daughter. Healing began for the family unit through these and other encounters.

Michaela added a comment about work. She overheard a school counselor talking with a youngster one day and noted how difficult that person's task was when compared with her job of teaching high school science. We laughed when we shared that the school counselor might make the same comment about Michaela's job. Michaela expressed satisfaction with each of the jobs performed at the site; she knew that just a simple comment could put a child at ease, and the smallest thing could wind up planting a seed for a child's later progress.

Michaela showed resilience by putting one foot in front of the other and solving problems as they came up. In finding activities that helped her relax, such as walking through the garden, she was better able to process all she faced over those years. Another great skill Michaela shared was being able to set aside certain tasks and concerns to take up other ones; a clear key to her success was her ability to go back and complete that earlier task.

⌖

Tess
"Contemplate and Then Take Action"

Tess learned early in life to develop boundaries, lean on herself, observe others, and to follow her own creative path. She was an entrepreneurial young woman who owned a beauty salon at the time of this interview.

Tess's mom was structured and asked about things like homework and everyday chores; she taught the children to follow through and get the job done. Her dad, on the other hand, was more philosophical. He talked with Tess about discovering inner talents and was able to listen to her stories at length. Tess talked with him about planning and then opening a business enterprise. All this energy went into it before it ever happened, it is just fine as it is now, and yet deliberate changes might happen in the near future. She knew more thought was required. Good health, a solid career, friends, and family; these are all a part of Tess's life at this time.

Tess talked about the creative spirit as her strongest part. It gets confusing, though, when some inside idea is brewing and it is not clear what it means for the present or for the future. Her advice to others is that if they are interested in the beauty business, it is important to study hard, obtain each applicable license, and gain some experience in each area before narrowing down their career choice. This variety in training will prove useful as a business needs to shift and change.

An earlier way Tess analyzed people was by studying their personalities. How they treated others; did they offer any contribution to the world? She chose a few people to watch closely.

It was not regarding their occupations; it was by studying their way of acting in the world and learning how they did things. She studied their behaviors to learn how she might fit in, to develop an individual style, and to find out what would work for her.

Tess had some trouble in her upbringing. A few family members considered her dad to be at risk for alcoholism. It remained unclear what they actually said or really meant. While their mom was at work, Tess and her sisters did what they were supposed to do—school work, chores, and keep each other company. They kept busy with whatever was on their mom's list. When their parents divorced, Tess and her siblings lived with each parent on some routine schedule, and they stayed with their grandparents now and then. Tess stayed out of all family quarrels. She learned how to care for herself as an individual, and she learned to care for her sisters. This time in her life contributed to the development of individuality and strength on the inside.

Tess also talked about setting goals, even small ones, and having things to work toward and to look forward to every day. A recently ended relationship had good and bad parts to it; it was all right for the present moment but not for a lifetime commitment. The split-up created a challenge, but it was essential. Each of them had to get past the attention they gave and received in the relationship; they had to trust themselves and each other enough to face whatever was insurmountable and make decisions that acknowledged their paths had diverged.

Tess stressed that it is important to face whatever one has to face. Living alone might be in her future; it might prove necessary for self-respect and well-being. In her mind's eye, making decisions and carrying them out are where strength comes from. The ability to be in touch with oneself on the inside is a gift. It is where the basis of decision-making comes from, especially when the decision affects a person's life. Tess's goal is for the reader to share this idea with others.

People sometimes lose themselves due to tensions in life. It is important to develop a balance between acting uncaring and overly dwelling on various issues, especially when it comes to family members. Her family knows about her listening ear; they also trust themselves to find their own way. It is important to remain an individual, to define and follow one's own path, and to do your best in moving forward. There are difficulties, accidents, trauma of some kind, and any of these can become a trigger for greater personal growth and understanding. People sometimes stand up for themselves with more confidence after living through a difficult event.

Tess's family often visits relatives in another part of the country. During one of these visits, it became obvious that her dad had pushed himself to a better life. He now shares more details of his early days, as well as how his goals are shaping up for his future. Tess did not realize she had brownish skin until she was almost in high school. Cultural education was not something the family focused on during her early years. In talking with relatives, she discovered their heritage includes at least five European countries, as well as the Native American culture. English was the family's main language throughout their history here.

Tess never identified as being from one culture. She was simply part of a family. Questions came up at times that were difficult to understand; this made her feel she did not belong. Her siblings wanted to know how to fit in, but Tess changed and grew not to have that concern, not to give it any thought. There were differences in Tess compared with others, and she grew to like herself for the person she became, which is one hundred percent American.

It is important for each person to learn to love and respect him or herself in order to keep growing in life. This is an essential feature of a healthy life, and it is necessary even when parents or other caretakers do not measure up to an ideal in a child's mind; no one is without shortcomings. We must learn to support ourselves, to stick up for ourselves, on deep levels. It is useful to learn to nurture the central part of ourselves; it might be all that we have for support at times.

Tess learned to look inside, make decisions, and go from there. A stable family life, even with its quandaries, helped this development. A willingness to think independently, outside the box, reflects inner strength and resilience that serves her well in life.

Vivian
"On Being Called Mom"

Vivian and I shared a private practice for many years. It was an exciting time for both of us when we started out with our newly granted marriage and family therapy licenses. We remain good friends and enjoy nearly annual visits.

The thing that stands out for me in terms of a before and after sequence is the event of my first daughter's birth. The circumstances surrounding it... has been an incredible journey in my soul... [She is] forty now. Back then, when I was pregnant with my first daughter, I was seventeen years old, her father was sixteen, and we were not in any position to get married. [This was a high school relationship.] We cared a lot about each other, but we were too young and there was... no family support and no support anywhere for helping us... to stay together and raise this child.

I was sent to a home for unwed mothers the last few months of my pregnancy, had the baby, and gave her up for adoption. Back then, there was no awareness on the part of birth mothers as to who adopted the child, where she lived, or anything about her. We were all enveloped in this web of judgment, of shame, and we were made to feel like we had no rights whatsoever... We were told uniformly not to worry about this, you'll have other kids, forget about this child, pretend it didn't happen, get on with your life.

I went back to high school, graduated, went on to college, and got on with my life... My parents were very good about acting like nothing had happened... It was never mentioned... [That secret equaled that I messed up, and I let the family down]... I was trying to find a place to feel that I was a... decent human being...

It kept me very much on my guard, quiet, don't say too much. I remember sitting with other women, young girls, women in college, talking about and wondering what it was like to have sex and have a baby. I knew but I couldn't say; I had to wonder along with them. Then I'd be in groups of women other times and they'd be talking and saying that they just didn't know how these women could give children up for adoption... I was not able to say anything. I was so trapped.

No one talked about keeping the baby in the family, and birth mothers are [advised] not to talk about it, so how could anyone know what they are going through... Nobody ever thought to ask, "What is it like for you?" They only talked about "look what you've done and this is what you have to do now."

It wasn't until birth mothers started speaking up that social service institutions took a second look at the damage they had done to the souls of the women they supposedly counseled. They didn't counsel them at all. For years, thirty years since my daughter was born, I lived with that secret... I don't believe that part of my soul was my own; it was split off... It was like that [for] thirty years of my life.

I remember reading an article in a paper about the ALMA Society—the Adoptees' Liberty Movement Association. It's a search organization about adoptees, birth mothers, etc. I cut that article out and put it away, hidden. It stayed hidden for another ten years, but I think this is when seeds were planted that maybe I could possibly [look for my daughter]. What would people think if I started looking for my daughter?

That processing went on under the surface... I was very isolated. It was like a contaminating toxin in my system, but I wasn't aware of it. If anyone had asked back then how [I handled it...], I would have said just fine... At that time, I was totally at peace with it... It just goes deep and it does not let the conscious mind know things. It took a long time for these things to penetrate my conscious mind.

[A big turning point happened during one of my first master's degree classes...] The woman who was running the class asked everyone to "Take out a paper and write down three things you've grieved for in life." I remember thinking I really haven't lost anything... [I thought longer.] Well, my grandmother died... my grandfather died. I remember losing a cat I really loved whose name was Tiger. The cat died when I was six years old. I remembered the grief of that as I was sitting there with my pencil and paper... So, I thought that's what I'll write, so I went to write 'cat' and I wrote 'child.' Just like that. I thought oh my God, this is very real. I just sat there and looked at it for the rest of class.

Pivotal things. I was in a seminar with this man doing groups. I had a feeling I should go in and talk with him individually... So, I made an appointment to go in and talk. One of the things I talked about was having this child; he was so supportive and listened. He asked, "Have you thought of finding her?" I [replied], "Oh no, I can't do that. I don't have any right to do that." He [commented], "You should think about that." I never thought of it like that; I just thought I was this terrible person and I don't have any right to go into my daughter's life. I never thought that it might be good for her to know me. That really started triggering more thinking about this... It shifted my perspective.

I told my sister [about the baby]. She was upset that she'd been kept in the dark, that our parents didn't tell her. I [explained to] her that it was not my idea. I felt very bad about it, but at that time, I felt there was nothing I could do. She [replied], "You could have said something earlier." Our parents have been dead a long time. I told her I know but I wasn't in a place where I could do that. Then she said, "We have a family member out there; why aren't you looking for her?" That's when I realized this loss wasn't just mine. My sister had lost a niece, my daughter had lost a sister, my son had lost a sister, my family had lost, and my whole clan had lost. I had not realized that.

After that, I talked with each of the children and my daughter said, "I have a sister out there; why aren't you looking for her?" My son didn't say that. He [commented], "This is very interesting. Very interesting." So, ten years later I pulled out that article. I was going to go to one [ALMA] meeting [and instead attended their national conference].

There I was with all these people, they had all these seminars, there were a lot of adoptees, and a lot of birth mothers. There were about thirty birth mothers in the caucus and we all started sharing our individual experiences. For the first time I realized that I'm not alone, we're all feeling the same way, and a good half or more had found their children.

Two women invited me to a search meeting at their house. That's when it started. It took ten months; there were two women who especially helped me. Just being able to do that and talk to some people about this experience started to lift that lid and shadow of secrecy. What I noticed was a freeing up of energy, a gathering of pieces of [me] that got left behind. I noticed feeling more empowered and not so afraid.

One of the things I did [at the beginning was that I] started talking to people. It was ten months and in February, I had my first daughter's phone number... It was a whole long process how that came about. I called her and had questions written out. I asked if she could talk for a while and she said no. She [suggested] calling back in about an hour. When I did, her husband answered and said she wasn't there. I was panicked. He was friendly. He said to call back in a while. He then gave me a time to call her back the following morning. "It's her turn to get up with the baby," he said.

I had a granddaughter! I had a very bad night. Brave me, is she gone? When I called the next morning, she wasn't there. Later she told me she knew who I was the minute she heard my voice, but she got scared. She needed time to process, so she went out to talk to a friend... and didn't know what to do. Then she decided to talk to me. She was torn between her adoptive mother and her curiosity. Her friend said, "You'll always wonder if you don't pursue this and see who this woman is."

It has been a transformation from what I was then to what I am now, in terms of this pivotal experience. My life is ongoing—being the mother of a child, having lost her for thirty years, and now she's been in my life for ten. I have grandchildren. This is just part of my life. My family has accepted that there's this extended family we have. It has given other dimensions to our relationship.

People's souls have tremendous powers of regeneration for healing and change. Our life's journey is so exciting. It's so important to, if we can, consciously have a little piece open to new possibilities, to new ways of looking at things. It does happen when we're not looking. There has to be a communication between the two parts. There has to be a bridge [as] you said. You have to believe that change is possible, that healing is possible...

From where I am now in my life... [I see so vividly the miracle] that makes change and healing possible. It's surprising because when I was going through the changes, I didn't have this awareness. Looking back, I can see advantages of getting older. You can see so much more looking back than you could when you were right there... [Things that were once so confusing might clear up in your mind's eye once you get past that particular stage in life.]

Probably the biggest message I want to leave is hope for healing wounds, growth, and change, reclaiming one's soul, and growing into one's soul and honoring it.

Vivian's ability to carry on with her life, to grow and change, even while keeping issues deeply inside that had no means of expression all those years, is a strong testimony to resilience.

Danny
"Quiet and Deep"

Danny worked with younger children at the time of this story. Using a soft-spoken approach, he had no trouble challenging behaviors as needed.

When Danny was little, his babysitter's younger siblings would come around, pick on, and bully him. He was a little kid who just stayed quiet, but he was confused and did not understand what to do. Danny could not see any reason why they picked on him.

He was upset, wounded on the inside, and felt stung by those blows. It was unconscionable to treat children that way, and it was appalling to hurt another person without provocation. Danny wanted neither to be in that position of inflicting pain, nor to be on the receiving end. He was all too familiar with what a devastating experience that could be.

Danny then talked about the breakup of his parents. This happened in his life during early elementary school. It took quite a while to understand that this situation was a long-term one. Mom told the boys about it, but to Danny it mostly meant that he, his brother, and his sister could sleep with their mom on certain nights. Danny's older brother understood more about what it meant for their futures.

Danny recognized that his dad was louder when arguments happened; it was his dad's fault because of that loudness. His mom was tearful, but at the time, he did not sense permanence. It still meant there were times when he and his siblings could jump into their mom's bed. His dad visited routinely during the day, but these did not include stay overs. It started to dawn on Danny during one of his dad's visits, however, that he really missed him. While running through the yard to hug his dad, Danny's eyes filled with tears and everything became blurry.

This particular day was a turning point for Danny on how to understand current family life. Fortunately, it started pleasantly for everyone. They visited throughout a good part of the day, and all the family members got along well. When Danny's dad started to say good-bye, Danny felt panicky. Among all family members, he was the only one crying. He felt strange and then the floodgates really opened up. Up until this moment in his young life, Danny thought you cried when you cut yourself or got hurt. Emotion was the word he used to describe these scenarios during our talk. What he went through just then was way over the edge, like a deluge. Danny did not say good-bye to his dad with the rest of the family. It was all too much. While hiding out in his room, he thought the family might think he had overdone the misery or the tears. It was later that he realized his reaction was perfectly normal for who he was at that time and age.

One of his teachers at that time was Miss L. She was aware of family circumstances and was the type of teacher who contributed to the self-esteem of her students. Miss L. chose Danny to help with chores a little more often than she chose other students who volunteered. Every time Danny helped her, he felt an increased sense of pride and self-worth. Those extra activities added a special meaning to his life. When the main assignment for the Christmas mural went to Danny, this meaning increased tremendously.

Danny showed up a little early for school and got to show off his artistry in working on particular parts of the display, including the reindeer and tree. The mural was on display throughout the school's Christmas events. He considered himself an average artist, but he felt confident about this contribution. Taking the responsibility his teacher offered gave Danny confidence, and it helped him find his place in the world. Being able to complete this task helped him know he could succeed with other challenges. In early elementary school years, this was significant.

Miss L. was able to take a small group of students on various outings that Danny often attended. He was excited when Miss L. made home visits. One day, Miss L. brought a real surprise; she cleaned out her house and gave him an old hockey stick. Although hockey had not been on Danny's agenda, he soon joined his fellow students in this new activity. That hockey stick provided a concrete connection point with Miss L.—that and various field trips he was able to join. Once she left on maternity leave, Danny behaved as a confident, successful student. The entire family was thrilled when Miss L. named her first son after him. The emotional bond with his mom had always been strong, and Miss L. provided an additional huge influence on Danny's development.

Starting in fifth grade, Danny found an identity—athletics. After sixth grade and beyond, sports meant a lot. Football and baseball made junior high school years go smoothly. Fast and accurate with moves, things went his way. It was easy to learn what to do; he had a gift and the skills came naturally. He shattered every record in high school, and along with athletic scholarships, he earned the title as the school's most outstanding athlete. College came next.

At age fifteen, Danny's dream was to give to someone else what Miss L. had given him. His sensitivity helped him see that need. His experience with Miss L., coupled with remembering quandaries and confusion about early childhood and babysitters, contributed to Danny's goal of wanting to 'be there,' wanting to put himself in a position to make a difference, to be able to keep others from going through the negatives he went through. Although he thought of becoming a teacher, his basic goal was to assist kids with their lives.

Danny geared himself for success in two ways. One was as an athlete; another was to advance his goal of working with children. He knew that a scholarship and college would help achieve those goals. His mom encouraged him to look into all kinds of scholarships, not just those related to sports. His grades were good enough for academic scholarships too. His mom's encouragement struck a chord in Danny that he keeps close even today. Her lesson was in that common phrase "Don't put all your eggs in one basket." Danny was both a good student and a strong athlete, though he looked at those traits as separate characteristics. He focused on and solidified a plan to be his best in all possible ways, so that in helping others society would benefit. Danny realized that to achieve these ideas success in life was necessary.

Because he knew what he wanted to do in life at a young age, Danny assumed other people knew their goals as well. Some friends mentioned professional interests but never followed up with training. Danny's own focus was clear about wanting to help children. Once while working with teens, he asked them a 'goals for their futures' question. The vast majority had no idea at all. Some wondered for themselves and had no answer, yet others were flippant and not interested.

At this time, Danny felt confident and passionate about a career in working with children—from younger than preschool up to the middle school age range. He had a gift in listening closely and being able to assist and mentor that age group. Danny found the right people for his own mentoring needs right at work. Sometimes he needed to change things around, not take them so seriously, and talking to people who were not directly involved in a given situation proved helpful. It pleased him that he saw these situations through from start to finish in work challenges.

Once Danny learned he was good at sports and athletics, he gained confidence to overcome earlier problems of bullying and the devastation of his parents' separation. Realizing he had academic skills, in addition to athletic ones, contributed to Danny's development of confidence and resilience. Strong support from his mom, coupled with a teacher who cued into needs and nudged him along in various ways, added to Danny's ability to achieve lifelong success.

Tricia
"On My Own at Last"

Tricia has been a close friend since early graduate school days. We have spent time together, traveled a bit, visited each other's families, and shared those millions of stories that only get better as years go on.

Life has thrown serious obstacles in Tricia's path, but gradually she found a way around them. Choices may not have always been best, but she made the most of every situation and corrected the course as needed. Tricia got married and had children at a young age. She may have married to get out of her childhood home. Her first child's birth contributed to depressive episodes, but no doctor was able to make any connection and really help. Things got worse until Tricia broke down and asked for help from her caring and life-saving grandmother.

With her grandma's financial help and moral support, Tricia saw a psychiatrist who used several aspects of treatment, including medication, and was able to see her through recovery. A favorite and close uncle killed himself with no warning the following year. Tricia felt she should have seen it coming, but she did not. This was difficult to reconcile, although with her grandma's continued help, Tricia was able to carry on and raise her toddler.

A second child was born; her husband started drinking and left her home alone with the children throughout the week. It became more than just a difficult situation, and before things got completely out of hand, Tricia packed up and headed to where her grandmother lived. She recognized the danger signs for herself and could see that the isolation due to her husband's ways was unworkable. Tricia's mother was there as well.

The family stayed together at her grandmother's house even after Tricia's husband flew out to be with them. It turned out that Tricia thrived in this new location. It was different from the small-town environment she had lived in. Anonymity was a relief in her mind's eye. She counted blessings, hoped her husband would drink less, and would contribute more to childcare. Tricia could carry on with some of her own life's interests here as well as care for the children. Her mom always had difficulty in expressing support and taking action, but Tricia could still feel that love for her and the children. Tricia's husband did continue drinking; this suddenly looked familiar in her experience because her dad drank too much.

Tricia and her husband separated several times through the years. At some point they bought a new home, their two children were in early school years, and they adopted a son. Two of Tricia's aunts cautioned her about problems with adoption. Even with actual difficulties that did arise, Tricia never regretted doing it. She and her husband were together at that point—calm and secure. She returned to school, took the required classes, and studied hard. She graduated with solid grades and was pleased with herself for that accomplishment.

When Tricia's mother and grandmother realized how well she was doing in school, they encouraged the thought of graduate school. That advanced training would help in earning a good living in the medical technician field. Money was not an issue at this time, but Tricia began questioning the marriage. She sensed something was not right. She learned of his cheating and decided enough was enough, or maybe even more than enough. Divorce came next.

Tricia's medical technician position pleased her to no end. It was second only to raising children. Her boss further encouraged an interest in graduate training. During that time, both at work and at school, people came into her life and remain there today as close friends.

Tricia maintains a belief in God, which seems to be a bit different from how she regards herself as a spiritual person. Both these factors mattered in getting over depression, asking for help at times, and even in a willingness to take medication once she decided it was necessary. Tricia believes this strength and courage did not come from home life but rather from a place deep inside.

Tricia's mom once talked about a great-great uncle who had abruptly committed suicide many decades prior, just as a close uncle had in recent years. Tricia changed this family dynamic, no matter how distant that dynamic was, by seeking help when necessary and going after goals without stopping. She also attributed some of this change and strength to God's intervention in her life.

Spirituality got her through many of life's difficulties. She readily bounces back, even when she does not necessarily see the whole problem clearly in the first place. Answers come to her. Tricia commented on how different people deal with stress. A change in the immediate environment often helps when stress gets to be too much. That does not mean leaving an area for good; it just means getting away for a while. Outdoor environments help, such as walking through a garden or going to the local park. Having coffee or tea with a good book in hand or meeting a friend is often rewarding as well. Staying playful on a regular basis, whatever that means at different times, is one of the best activities for good health—physical, mental, and emotional.

Tricia found ways to move forward regardless of how difficult it was at times. She persevered through many trials and came out on top. Asking for help and accepting it from her grandmother led to a route for developing resilience later in life. Thinking independently is another strength that helped with the next challenge, whatever it turned out to be. Recognizing God and her personal spirituality played an important role and contributed to Tricia's mental and emotional health and well-being. The man currently in Tricia's life is upbeat and enthusiastic, especially in seeking ways for her to laugh and play. His caring is evident, and in turn, he shared that caring for her has helped his own life more than anything else has.

Noelani
"Marching Right Along"

Noelani and I went to graduate school together and often shared stories back and forth.

Noelani shared descriptions of images that repeatedly showed up in her mind's eye. These images included tall ceilings, stained glass windows, and she sometimes wondered about out-of-body experiences, as she seemed to peer down from the top of the ceiling onto weird scenes. People wore tall masks, head decorations, and dark clothes, and they lined up and stood tall on the ground floor.

There seemed to be a connection between these images and scary dreams, during which Noelani felt that her dad's life was threatened. He needed protection, so she kept quiet about any fears or unsettling issues that floated through her head at times. No mention of these images or fears occurred until years later. A question arose from deep within her psyche about a church link, but it remained unanswered.

Noelani used many avenues to face these issues. As a youngster, she worked at making jewelry and writing poems. She scribbled random weird-looking designs and wrote prose. Two teachers requested after-school help from Noelani. Just about every student enjoyed helping teachers at school. This added a bit of extra attention and one more activity to her daily life. Noelani credits a strong family life with helping her focus on school, as well as biking, reading, library trips, and other productive enterprises. This family support rings true in her mind's eye, even though it was much later in life when she mentioned even a tiny bit of these weird dreams and ideas to any family member. She eventually picked one brother, one cousin, and one friend to talk with about these nightmares. These visits and talks contributed to her healing process.

Dreams provided healing throughout Noelani's early years. A couple of dreams went on for decades, on and off. In one of them, she dreamed that death would come at a particular age. After actually surviving that specific birthday, Noelani faced a type of rebirth. She went into therapy, studied, and participated in Gestalt, sand tray, and other active therapy approaches. They helped her to find her way through and past any negative focus. She learned about mindfulness, living in the present tense, and letting go of past issues. It involved a lot of practice, fresh starts, and time.

Noelani also talked about a different recurring dream. In this dream, a friendly coffee shop way out in the country provided an opening scene. The person fixing coffee for others wore bright colors. She kept an upbeat attitude toward the guests, regardless of whether she later led them, one at a time, out a secret passageway or back through the main door of the building. Guests never seemed to know that individuals among them went out two separate exits. The exit that continues the story was a secret passageway. The challenge for people leaving through that passageway was to get through a dark, stuffy tunnel filled with obstacles, eventually emerging out in the open in one piece. Once those folks made it outdoors, they found sunshine, blue skies, and a completely new life ahead. Over time, this dream became so familiar to Noelani that it was more like an adventure, and she eventually realized that she was the one making her way to a better life.

A strong relationship with teachers, a sound home life, and the ability to carry on with schoolwork, especially in times of worry and distraction, are features of resilience. Noelani's early involvement in crafts, baking, reading, and biking helped with focus and kept her moving forward.

Steve
"Stable and Steadfast"

Early and sudden death in the family provided a key turning point in Steve's life. He worked in the education field for a number of years.

The past twenty to thirty years made a huge difference in Steve's life. Things shifted dramatically for him and his family when they suffered the loss of two family members within a short time. An uncle died in his mid-fifties and a cousin died of cancer as a teenager. Prior to their illnesses, Steve's uncle worked hard for both families; it was just his way. Their properties adjoined; he worked at his regular job, and he was the main builder and fix-it person around their homes. His cousin was an athlete and excelled in academics. Steve thought that moms who worked at home worked as hard as people who worked away from home. Hard-working people were there every day of his life.

Before the family members became ill, Steve focused on anything but school. When he took community college classes, there were no educational goals or career plans in mind. He worked at odd jobs of all sorts, one at a time, and always did his best. Examples were car oil changes, miscellaneous repair jobs, and assisting on tour trips. As long as he worked hard and was successful every day, he was satisfied. That work ethic came directly from his parents and close relatives. At the time, it did not translate to completing any college program or setting a long-term career goal.

Steve was startled beyond words once both family members died. Their deaths woke him up with a deep internal shudder. Something was not quite right about his own life, and suddenly it became obvious. A big shift was about to happen. Steve's family accepted whatever lifestyle pattern suited him; they trusted him to find his way. Education was valued but not placed above other interests. His dad and uncle expressed enthusiasm for his sporting events just as they did for a strong academic grade. The freedom for Steve to choose his own path seemed to be more important to his family than his education. Nonetheless, formal education was about to materialize for him.

Steve went into the education field knowing that family members who passed before him were somehow aware of this change in lifestyle. They were unable to develop as much as they might have, had they lived longer, and perhaps they wanted more from him in his present life. Steve wondered about these relatives, and he wondered what they would say about how far he had gotten in his current life since the time of their deaths.

Steve lives with an overall optimistic attitude about life. A dark cloud has an edge of bright light that shows up if one looks closely enough. As bad as those deaths were, they provided a trigger to a different level of living for Steve and his family. Following the difficulties they endured because of these deaths, Steve's remaining family members found themselves more alive. They became acutely aware of those among them who still had opportunities that those who died had lost. They set aside the choice of negatives and complaints and chose to go forward with renewed energy and goals.

Steve commented on being thirty at his college graduation, and in an obvious contrast to the past, he has been in the same field for many years. He shares this story about his own shifts in focus when talking with friends about their kids. He tells these friends how it was for him, how he had no real idea about which way to turn. Steve encourages these friends to let their sons and daughters experience life, to grow at their own pace, in their own way, and to trust that they will eventually find their way. Once a concrete idea emerged about how to proceed in life, he was able to develop and accomplish goals without any trouble.

Steve had a lot to say in encouraging people to go to and remain in college—even if they are not sure what they want to do—because that experience can contribute to a positive attitude and a strong foundation. This idea also includes certificate or licensed training programs following high school. This is a better route than not going to college or having other training at all. Education beyond high school is a better choice, he emphasized, even when a person goes back for more training or for an entirely different program later.

Sometimes a strong focus allows a person to finish goals rapidly, and other times people face situations where plans don't work out regardless of how hard they worked. This requires willingness, openness, plus an ability to investigate further; it sometimes forces them to choose differently or redevelop a plan from scratch.

There are times when you can find a completely different way to solve a problem than you first thought possible. It may take more than one time around; you may have to start fresh and forge a different route. It is important to keep going, to put one foot in front of the other.

Steve went through several transitions throughout early adulthood years. Whatever his enterprise was at the time, he showed independence in thought and action. This reflects resilience encouraged by his family. At the time of the family deaths, resilience appeared both in uniting the family and in the fact that each family member found the courage to renew his or her individual path.

Daphne
"Heal from the Roots Up"

Daphne was highly successful in the medical field and raised several children. She engaged in arts and crafts projects and sold her work at local fairs.

Daphne looks back at childhood now and then. The amount of traveling the family participated in almost became like wandering a different planet. She gained resilience by having to adapt to the family's daily or weekly location changes, but she would not wish that lifestyle on anyone. The children attended school in a variety of states before they settled in one area for any length of time. They missed a sense of security and routine.

The family did not follow a set route; it was often by chance that they wound up in some specific spot. Available jobs made a difference, and their dad was good at many different tasks. Sometimes a bad storm caused enough damage that he worked in one area repairing buildings for a week or two. Churches were often generous when the family asked for help, and sometimes work became available directly through them.

Her parents were troubled; sometimes her dad seemed desperate in her young eyes. Credit was not easy and they were not in a position to handle being in debt for even a minute. They often went without. They traveled during an era when small towns allowed credit for a week at a time while a person worked at an odd job. Once the week ended, it was time to settle the credit or pay it back. The family was large, which sometimes made matters worse. For example, they had a tight squeeze in one car. If the family kept their own school records, it would have been helpful, but it did not turn out that way. Confusion reigned every time they started at a new school.

Mom was a normal, loving mom, and Daphne received a good foundation from her in spite of the time spent on the road. Desired stability simply was not possible with this lifestyle, and many times Daphne felt her dad had a scary personality. The family seldom seemed calm. Chilling and tense moments happened often between her parents. Daphne feared that something awful would happen. She wondered if her dad had control of himself at times. One specific incident was when their table 'accidentally' tipped over with food on it. At other times, he seemed solid. She worried about both parents. Domestic violence was a high risk. Alcohol was not an issue, but her dad was often on edge.

The family wound up at a church plenty of times. Mom would

go in to speak to the priest with one child in tow. There were mixed reactions; some conversations were friendly and helpful, but at other times, Daphne could not wait to leave. Dad would be in or near the car, possibly on a bench waiting for them to return. Different children joined their mom on different days; the smell of good food and the sight of fine furniture were two things Daphne vividly remembered about many of these visits.

Something changed during one period. The family stayed put and the children attended the same school for more than one week or one month. The priest who hired Daphne's dad found a way to talk with her parents. He needed helpers on the church grounds, knew of odd jobs available in town, and even located a small house for them to live in. For a time, this seemed heaven-sent. At school, Daphne made friends, passed her classes, and advanced. The family participated by completing school cleaning chores in exchange for the routine contribution of food and clothing.

In switching to speak about marriage, things changed right after the wedding ceremony. She had initial doubts about the relationship, but the change in her husband was so sudden that it made her wonder who she married. The man who was attentive and caring now blamed her for whatever ailed him, and he blamed everything on her childhood. He tried to get her to see a doctor and wanted her on meds. He pushed her to cook a certain way, wear certain clothes, and he could be mean and demanding about it. There were no hassles at home as long as Daphne followed her husband's plan in every detail. Annulment became a possibility at that time.

The next minute, he would change his approach, say kind instead of mean things, and would talk positively about their progress together. One good thing that remained consistent throughout married life was that the children lived in a good home, attended good schools, and grew up in one neighborhood. Daphne attended home games, school programs, and all the rest. Suddenly her husband stopped taking an active role in family life and became too tired for even ordinary conversations. Things went downhill after that, but alcohol and drugs stayed out of the picture. Daphne knew it would not help to dwell on the past; it was important to continue with plans to move forward. Her husband thought they would remain married, she would continue doing what he asked, and that would be that.

Daphne did see a doctor; therapy was the doctor's recommendation. The therapist encouraged further education. The idea of her husband attending a therapy session went nowhere. Regarding educational goals, she had been hesitant to take the harder medical classes; her confidence needed building. As it turned out, she aced just about every class related to medicine; in at least one case, she received higher grades than any student had ever received. That turned out to be a strong confidence booster.

With several children in tow, plus school, Daphne was busier than ever, but she was thrilled with her accomplishments. A plan was necessary if something was going to work for everyone. Daphne studied art and medicine while her children were young.

Once divorce entered the picture, she went for it almost immediately after finishing basic education. She knew she could earn a living. Her husband did not believe the divorce would happen, and he did not take any action until months later. At that time, she told him what she had learned about child custody and how she planned to rearrange the house. He would have to sleep on the couch; she was taking over the bedroom and was no longer sleeping in the attic. He left soon after. They had a prior arrangement that allowed her to keep the house; the children would spend time with each parent, and they would live mainly with their mom.

Daphne mentioned her mom again. During her growing up years, and even in adulthood, Daphne did not feel anger toward her mom; rather, she felt care and concern for her. Her mom's own childhood was less than desirable. Sometimes her mom spoke as if

Daphne, a child, knew the answers, but she was far too young to have any real idea. She did listen, though, and this probably helped her mom more than she ever realized.

Daphne dreaded telling her mom about the upcoming divorce. The family liked him, so she expected resistance. Yet when the time came, Daphne received support and encouragement. Her mom went on to talk about how she, as the mom, did not support Daphne enough during childhood. She felt bad about this, expressed sorrow, and apologized. She acknowledged that what Daphne went through was absolutely one hundred percent unacceptable.

Daphne felt an incredible relief when her mom made comments about that responsibility in her early life. The relief was so tremendous that Daphne acknowledged that perhaps at an earlier time she had been angry with her mom after all. Daphne and her mom continued with their strong relationship.

Another story was about her dad. During adulthood, Daphne reached a stage in life where processing all the issues was complete enough on the inside to tell her dad that she forgave him for all his errors in her life. There was neither need nor desire to carry that burden around any longer. It had become an energy drain. Daphne expressed everything that was necessary, and she was grateful that he was still alive to hear her words. He looked teary-eyed and did not say much aloud, but Daphne knew from his expression that he knew exactly what she meant.

Her dad lived to a ripe old age. Daphne's mom became his caretaker. Daphne's dad had been quite ill and weak toward the end of life; his frailty bothered him more than anything else did. It took time after his death for her mom to grieve. Her mom has lived well and had many happy years following her husband's death. Daphne used writing as closure once her dad died.

∞

Resilience for Daphne and siblings started at an early age. She showed inner strength, and adapted and developed the flexibility required given the family's lifestyle. Daphne's mom was another factor in the development of resilience. Her continued love and caring throughout the years meant a lot, even with her shortcomings and the excessive travels. Taking steps in education toward art and medicine, as well as her eventual divorce, reflect Daphne's abilities in decision-making, strength, and courage of heart.

Elyse
"New and Different"

Elyse earned a living as an aesthetician and worked in research on her own time. Nutrition and health products were part of a favorite research project.

Elyse started out talking about divorce. At the beginning, it often feels completely overwhelming and it can be devastating for some people. Eventually, that tunnel of despair lightens up and there is a chance, an opening, for renewed light, for a new life. Things change along the way, and the children act differently. Elyse taught her children to try hobbies and find some they liked. At first, they questioned their mom about what was so important about hobbies, and later they talked with increased understanding about the value of hobbies and other activities. The focus required for any particular activity makes all the difference. It forces your mind to some place specific and gets it away from trouble spots. Whenever the children engaged in hobbies together, it proved especially valuable because it gave them a time and place to talk together and to let go of things that were bothering them.

Elyse mentioned how fast time goes by. She has been at her current salon for several years without even realizing it. Her focus on work, research, workouts, children, and grandchildren all help with past issues. A new interest in vitamins and minerals is beneficial to mental energy right now; research shows that a particular product is good and has science behind it. Elyse did say, however, that she would not want to become a distributor, although she is willing to talk about these products with others. Elyse has geared her work toward skin care and has given up styling hair; she keeps too busy to do both.

Divorce was mutual, though there was some hassle about custody during the early days. When looking back now, she wonders why divorce was so overwhelming and why she, her family, and friends put so much energy into divorce and custody issues. Eventually, things worked out. Now the children are all young adults and are on their own. She and her ex continue to see each other at special occasions, which work out all right. Both of them continue to live in the same area and have known the same people for years. Elyse said that sometimes life goes this way. There is school, friendship, romance, marriage, children, and then a change happens.

Finally, divorce, and the issues surrounding it, ended and that was that. There was probably no reason for so much concern about it in the first place. The beginning days were difficult, especially with children. As time went on and different things happened, Elyse settled down, regained focus, and moved forward again. Grandchildren are in her life now, and she is grateful about that. There is concern about certain friends who feel they need marriage, and when divorce happens, they are vulnerable and possibly at great risk. They might make a mistake, not see things clearly, and find themselves caught up in some relationship that is not beneficial to either one. It is important for them to understand that they do not need a husband or wife, even if they grew up thinking otherwise. They are capable of stepping away from it all, making a different choice, and simply standing on their own two feet.

Elyse cherishes different types of books and finds stress relief through reading. Topic choices vary. Cooking and baking are fun, although she gives away most of her baked goods. Otherwise, there would be too much food at home! Elyse occasionally attends church. Grandchildren go with her now and then, and there is an appreciation for the strong foundation that church helps build. She brought up her own children in the Catholic Church, and now she visits a variety of churches with friends. It would not be all right to interfere with children's choices about religion, and church attendance, once they become adults.

Several grandchildren live in the area, which makes holidays more than busy. In addition, Elyse invites grandchildren for overnight or weekend visits. The schedule allows for one or two grandchildren at a time; this gives each of them a chance for a more personal visit. It certainly makes for an active family life.

Elyse engaged in a variety of activities through difficult times, which helped her remain strong and capable. Deliberate activity helps relieve stress and makes it possible to move in a positive direction toward solving problems and making good decisions. Elyse taught her children and teaches her grandchildren the same techniques, thus building resilience throughout the family.

SEVEN

Derek
"Ten Acres and Family Support"

D erek is quite clear about stating that his family's move to ten acres provided a huge turning point in his life. He worked in the information technology (IT) field in an educational setting for a number of years.

Derek came from a small farming community. Both his parents had many siblings. Family life, out of necessity, was highly structured; most tasks had to be finished together. In elementary school, he and his siblings were the only black students. It was a mixed bag for them; sometimes it was fine, other times it was no fun at all. They learned to take care of themselves early in life. Overall, they liked that school. A large extended family provided plenty of children to play with, as well as good-sized family get-togethers. Early in elementary school, his family bought a home on ten acres. That was Derek's home until college; one of the biggest changes for him was that in the new setting he attended a school with mostly black students.

Lawyers, doctors, as well as other professionals, lived in that area, and Derek now lived among upper middle-class black folks. School transition proved easy. His dad worked as an engineer, and his mom was a nurse practitioner. Their ten-acre farm was mainly a hobby farm. Derek drove a tractor before ever driving a car. He also drove a Chevy pickup truck, although he drove both the truck and tractor only around the ten acres at first. Derek made a joke about how well cars and trucks held up in those days; he used that common phrase about how "they don't build them like that anymore."

His job was to set the example for his siblings and be the responsible one. His family experienced plenty of tragic moments over time. Coming from quite a large family of her own, his mom lost several siblings at a young age. This forced Derek, his siblings, and their cousins to come to grips with death while they were quite young. His parents were supportive of their children. They made an effort to explain things and help their children understand. Derek loved to take things apart, and whenever he needed help putting them back together, his dad would step in and show him how to do it. Curiosity remained high; with family support and encouragement, he explored and tinkered with a large variety of items throughout those early years.

Derek talked about both earlier life in the tougher area and the ten-acre life, as he referred to it. Students from elementary school days, now high school age, sometimes geared themselves toward negative behaviors; they were in trouble already, and in some cases, they were in jail or dead. That old neighborhood was tough plenty of times. The ten acres brought a certain isolation, which, along with sports, made a positive difference in Derek's life. Sports drew him in, and sometimes Derek's dad was the only dad there to watch a game or other sports activity. He was grateful that his dad's professional position made it possible for him to attend. He saw himself able to go either way in behaviors, and family support made all the difference.

Derek's dad belonged to community groups connected to supporting children. Fundraisers at main holiday times were a prime example, such as Christmas trees and fireworks on the Fourth of July. Derek did his best to join his dad at all times; this resulted in him gaining experience working with children while he was still quite young. Derek referred to his dad as special, and he mentioned that they got along well, first as father and son and secondly as two adults. They often talked over a variety of issues together. Both seemed to benefit. His mother was the family's anchor. She provided a soothing aspect to her children's lives, and at the same time, she was knowledgeable and capable of many accomplishments.

In reflecting back on those earlier years, name-calling was common enough for that age group; Derek learned at a young age not to believe the names and not to take any of it seriously. He felt challenged to think about the future, and he referred to this time as the time for him to shape survival skills as they related to his attitude. Partly, this meant internal decisions about his approach to people, challenges, how he would get along with others and face the world as an adult. He also learned how to defend himself physically. Once he demonstrated that ability a few times, he rarely had to repeat it.

He stayed at his grandmother's after school now and then. She was interesting and old-fashioned in some ways. As almost a second mom, she made the effort to teach Derek about many things and gave him ideas to ponder and learn about. He commented again about his ten acres life. The changes that were abrupt regarding this move included school, home, activities, and chores. It made life a lot better. He saw himself as somewhere between passive and aggressive, and during his younger years, he attended different schools; his family looked for the right environment for him. Once on the ten acres, school life, along with everything else, improved. New friends had a similar home background and more in common with him.

Although books and sports were top on the list at that time, Derek did mention that girls started noticing him. Reading was a favorite activity, and it was helpful that the mobile library stopped on his street. His sports ability improved with every practice. Summer camp was a great experience in Derek's life; he learned about rowing and swimming, as well as arts and crafts. He made friends with several other students in attendance, and he summed it up by saying that his social skills seemed to develop along with the crafts.

Derek continues to keep in touch with some friends he made while at summer camp. During years of attendance, it was fabulous to explore the wilderness and participate in hikes. Youngsters who attended made inquiries and swapped stories about each other's home life, school happenings, and lifelong dreams. His own children are curious and ask quite a few questions about their family history. It has been a pleasure to tell them stories. The favorite story is about his move to the ten acres; he shares every detail about the move itself, as well as how much it meant to him.

Before sixth grade, one incident resulted in the shooting death of a young relative who visited with his family that day. This tragedy happened in the blink of an eye and brought distress to the family for quite a long time. The event made a lasting impression on Derek about life and death; it taught him how quickly things change. This memory was all the stronger because the person who died was close to his own age.

Another family difficulty was about his grandfather. From the time his grandfather collapsed and fell to the ground, several minutes elapsed before the emergency medical technicians [EMTs] arrived to assist him. His situation was so severe that the EMTs were barely able to revive him long enough for the family to gather to say good-bye. The damage done was far beyond repair. Derek's grandfather lived just a few more days, which was a blessing in Derek's mind. Hospice arrived, which helped the family prepare and accept the situation. He believed it would have been far worse if his grandfather had continued to live, both for him as well as for the rest of the family. Several months earlier, his grandfather thought he might have had a stroke. This idea remained completely hidden until a family member asked him what had happened to his hand. He did not want to burden the family; he was a strong character and role model. Derek thought it would be best for the family to remember him that way.

Derek spoke of another thing he learned during this family episode. Paramedics must work to revive a person unless a do-not-resuscitate order is in place. This was a creepy thought once it was realized how much damage had happened in apparently just a few minutes. His grandmother knew that the end was close for his grandfather, but it had not quite happened yet. It was especially difficult on her. Although some relatives were grateful to have a day or so to arrive and say good-bye, Derek thought the family could say good-bye in other ways.

His parents taught their children to respect others and not to discriminate toward people or races. His marriage to an Italian woman occurred in an outdoor setting; both sets of families accepted this union. Sometime later, Derek received a letter of excommunication from the church his family had attended for decades. Words in that letter suggested inappropriate behaviors. The family understood that those comments related to his choice of marriage partner, as well as having the wedding in an outdoor setting. In short order, family members quit the church one after another. A thorn in family life developed because of that letter. It annoyed them that church hierarchy took over after a family member made a small comment about the beauty of the wedding.

In Derek's way of thinking, God and church are separate. Church is there for some learning but mainly for fellowship. No church should have the kind of response to a wedding that his former church had. His anger lasted a long time, and it was even longer before he ever set foot in a church again. Years later, he and his wife found a nondenominational church that he irregularly attends. This new church, even though teaching many of the same words, stays away from rules and strictness. This is a stark contrast to Derek's old church, which he claimed survived on inflexibility.

He made an interesting comment about race by disclosing extended family comments. Relatives have suggested that because Derek's own family is somewhat lighter than they are, his family will have an easier time with acceptance. Derek's family tells them over and again just to let that thought go. They say that challenges exist regardless of color and regardless of other issues. His parents taught him and his siblings to be enterprising people and to take initiative and responsibility for their own lives. They have a solid education backing them; they face the world with an optimistic attitude. Derek and his wife teach these values to their children; one of their goals is that these values will trickle down through the generations to the larger population.

Derek's story demonstrates resilience in a number of ways. One way comes directly from the family's value system, which he later taught his children. Hard work, along with a positive outlook on life, helps people overcome many obstacles they encounter. Physical activities, such as hikes at camp and involvement in sports at a young age, are additional factors that reinforce resilience.

Cindy
"On My Own"

Cindy developed resilience in life through setting boundaries and pushing herself forward. One example of those boundaries was the refusal to tolerate drugs in her home. She has had a varied career, and at the time of this talk, she worked with children in after-school activities.

We had only a short time for this particular talk; Cindy offered to talk about her first boyfriend as well as career development. She spent a summer between college semesters in a small town at her brother's place. They attended a festive community celebration where one of his friends played in the band, and introductions happened during the break. Cindy and this friend took one long look at each other and decided to date.

Each of them planned to attend college in different parts of the state, so they formed a long-distance relationship that started during the fall semester. Letters and poetry went back and forth. Many friendships readily developed during Cindy's time here, and some of those same people remain close with her today. These early friendships helped curb some loneliness Cindy felt as part of the long-distance relationship. There was one complication about this new relationship. His family lived in the same small town; Cindy felt his mother did not care for her. It was possible that his mother had already chosen her son's bride in her own mind. The next thing Cindy knew, this new boyfriend went off to war. Although frantic, she chose to keep a stiff upper lip and get through each day by keeping busy, visiting friends, and just doing her best. Her impression was that people expected her to be down and negative day and night. That was no way to live; she continued with a plan geared for success and learning. Nighttime arrived and there was no way to deny the feelings that went with constantly missing him and continual worry. Only one close friend shared in this part of her story.

They married shortly after his return. Her husband wanted to return to school, so they moved to a different university town in time for the upcoming semester. His stated goal was to study, get a degree, and carry on with life. Cindy got a job and took classes in this new town. There was worry about how differently her husband acted after he returned home, but Cindy noticed changes in herself as well. While he was gone, she worked, kept things going, and felt like the boss.

Living together during all of this was upsetting. He signed up for but did not attend many classes; instead, visits with friends at the university's center on campus occupied his time. Cindy continued with classes and worked as the sole breadwinner. It was wearing; her husband became edgy and somewhat disrespectful. Emotional abuse became a risk. Neither of them accurately anticipated how difficult his readjustment would be.

A description of tension at various parties added background to her story. This tension arose because at times too many of her husband's friends stood too close to Cindy. She did her best to brush this off by simply stepping away. Although she did not talk about it for some time, it was troublesome. Her husband seemed to crave socializing at these parties; they agreed to set aside time to visit with each other for a few minutes every hour. Something still seemed off to Cindy. She contributed to an already confusing situation by trying to fix everything, by trying to solve it all with a magic wand. She asked herself about errors and thought about how to do better. This increased any self-imposed pressure on her already busy life, which took a while to see. Her husband was upset about not having a job and not contributing financially at all. There was more to this story, but Cindy did not know about most of it at the time.

It was important not to throw in the towel without giving the relationship time during those early years. A few years later, however, Cindy filed for divorce. They divorced and then got together again within several months. Cindy knew he had an awful time while away at war, which contributed to her willingness to start over. The courtship began again with poetry and letters. A son was born and they both wanted to make the family work. It did not last. Each time they married, they remained married for the same number of years and married on the same national holiday.

Once she and her husband divorced for the second time, Cindy went back to school for a college degree. Immediately following graduation, a completely different opportunity opened up. While tutoring some children next door who attended school with her son, their mother asked if she could help assist with minor political activities, such as stuffing envelopes. This led to participating in a visit from the president to the local area.

Cindy wound up with enough photos and articles for a scrapbook. She was at the airport to greet the president. While she volunteered to answer phones on another occasion, the White House called. Cindy briefly dated a staff person who worked for the president, and she attended various local functions to listen to the president speak. It was a thrilling time of life. In getting involved with the election of judges, Cindy spoke to both small and large groups; public speaking helped her gain self-assurance in other aspects of life. These activities were not on any prior list of goals, but she took advantage of clear opportunities and gained everything she could from this time in life. The experiences coincided with the time of Cindy's college graduation; these two events marked an important time in her life and signified a huge upswing in her confidence level.

Cindy talked about a similar type of development that happened regarding juvenile custody. At first, she worked as a clerk typing out forms. Things shifted in that field, and Cindy wound up gaining a large variety of experiences, none of which matched her initial expectations about the job. All this occurred shortly after college; teaching jobs were not readily available. For a while, Cindy earned income by cleaning houses and later worked as a secretary. One particular secretarial job paid the bills, but that was all. The work was not desirable; fortunately, she soon switched to a different position.

One day, Cindy visited a friend who worked in a lawyer's office. Their workload was enormous, and as soon as the lawyers realized that Cindy was a good typist, they asked her to accept a job. She switched right over; this move was a good fit for all involved. Later, when her friend left that law practice, Cindy received an instant promotion to fill that position. It proved to be a tremendous experience in her life. She received training in paralegal work and succeeded quite well with those challenges, along with the various management and organizational tasks she undertook. This position lasted a number of years, kept Cindy busy, and proved to be an education in itself. Her attitude was positive toward working hard right along with the rest of the group.

Cindy often felt that the things that happened in her life just came to her; it was not by choice. Her attitude connects to the old saying "What did not kill her would make her stronger." The other old saying mentioned was "God does not give her anything more than she can handle." She was proud that she found a way through or around life's obstacles. She learned to laugh at herself; once she did, things lightened up and she did not take everything so seriously. Things do have a way of working out for the better once you look back at them.

Cindy learned to set boundaries along each of the steps of life. She faced reality in light of her husband's post-military adjustment issues. Cindy's inquisitiveness and willingness to explore are features of resilience. When she combined those two aspects of life with an attitude that hard work and completion of tasks were important, she found a way forward that suited her best.

Sierra
"Church and Community"

Sierra and I have been good friends for a long time. She has worked for many years as a college English teacher and professional writer.

Sierra shared bits and pieces of stories from a recent reunion. Prior to that segment of our talk, she mentioned that her dad was a church minister. As a youngster, she was enthusiastic about his work because she knew his parishioners appreciated him. He did a great job in the counseling aspects of his duties; he seemed to have a natural gift in that direction regardless of the age or gender he counseled. In early adult years, Sierra heard a story from a friend about a marriage counseling session. Her friend, Kaelin, was confused and concerned about marrying outside her church.

Kaelin told Sierra that her dad brought in an easel with blank chart paper. He told Kaelin she could use this paper in any way that would help clarify things in her mind and in her heart; for example, she could write a list, draw, or scribble. He even suggested tearing a sheet into pieces, shaping origami characters, and having the characters talk with each other! Sierra's dad taught Kaelin to notice various pros and cons involved, see what mattered more, and notice what was less important. Looking at the relationship as it is now and then projecting different scenarios about the future would help. This would take time; Sierra's dad did not push one way or the other. After hearing Kaelin's story, Sierra appreciated that her dad helped Kaelin make up her own mind and go from there. Church pressure did not enter the picture.

A friend of Sierra's dad, a deacon in a different church, shared a different church story. That particular church gathered enough funds to purchase and maintain a van, which they used to pick up homeless people and drive them to an outreach program for a hot meal; sometimes a church member drove the van to bring food directly to where the people were staying. This same church also received a house donated from a member at the time of his death. This home became a shelter for teens going through difficulties. At some point, this program connected to a larger community program that included school, training, and jobs for teens.

Sierra sometimes felt confused about her dad's work when she was a child; he was involved for many days and nights in a row during special church events. Those occasions took him away from his family; preparing sermons involved several hours per week, in addition to the millions of other things he did for the church. At the same time, it was fun to listen to his sermons, and Sierra felt happy when parishioners seemed to appreciate and sometimes act on his words. She heard about his leadership in church matters while eating cookies after the service. It was fun to have those delicious treats on Sunday mornings!

At the reunion, Sierra heard many stories. Her friend Dennis talked about churches from other parts of the country that are enormous with thousands of people in attendance on weekends. These churches often have a large variety of groups with activities for all ages; they sometimes have over a hundred different ministries going on at the same time. As an adoptee, when someone unexpectedly contacted her about a possible family connection, Dennis's wife was grateful to have an adoptees group at their church to turn to for information and support. Dennis said there were groups on just about any topic one could imagine.

A young man and a young woman shared stories with Sierra's aunt as she arranged brochures and fixed coffee for reunion attendees; both stories shared a highly unusual perspective. The young man, George, felt sure from a young age that he was going to become a priest. His family, skeptical at first, eventually supported his choice to study toward that lifestyle. Things went well with his studies during the first year or so. However, in the middle of that training, something bothered George to a greater and greater extent. Quandaries increased, but he kept it all inside. It caught up with him while he was home visiting his family during the summer. Although he hardly spoke a word of this, he came to see that too large a number of fellow students were 'in it' for their future popularity and fame, not for any deep interest in the religious aspects of church. This atmosphere did not sit well with him and caused many nights of anxiety and worry. By summer's end, George consulted with a professor and arranged for an abrupt, quiet departure. When he eventually married and raised a family, they attended services together in their new area.

The young woman then shared a story with Sierra's aunt. This young woman, Gladys, said that although there were many enjoyable aspects of early convent life, she left and returned several times over the years for various reasons. As a teacher, Gladys found a strong connection with younger and middle school students. She did so well with lessons that the director asked for her help in developing certain aspects of the curriculum. Her students enjoyed the hands-on science projects she brought in weekly. She continued to teach at the younger levels, tutor certain college classes, and attend church.

Lilibeth, a close friend of Sierra's, continued their reunion visit with a chat about hometown life during their youth. They appreciated the communities where they grew up. Following Sierra's story about her dad as a minister, Lilibeth talked about her dad as a volunteer ambulance driver in her hometown. From European descent, he became close friends with the highly regarded police chief of African-American descent. These two men first became acquainted on emergency calls. On other occasions, they talked and laughed about how they were raising their children to stay in school, get good educations, and make good lives for themselves. Their children attended the same schools; church attendance meant going to one of the two or three churches in the area. People worked hard and got along with each other. Mutual respect across the board was obvious.

Sierra summarized by saying that she and Lilibeth agreed with each other about how much their parents' lives and community attitudes helped shape their own lives toward hard work, responsibility, and respect. These features of resilience helped them make sound decisions and wise moves in their lives.

∞

Rachelle
"Life with My Brothers"

Rachelle worked with younger children at the time she shared this story.

As a child, Rachelle had some faith in God and in exploring nature. She lived a carefree life and was free to play outdoors with siblings and friends. She loved animals, especially horses, and made up many stories about travel; she often included these animals in her imaginative tales.

Disruption happened abruptly for Rachelle's parents, which resulted in their separation. This went on and off for a while, then months went by without either parent visiting the other. This situation caused a lot of confusion and secret worry. Several months later, Rachelle's mother visited them while at the airport, and she talked about her plan not to return home but instead to live temporarily with relatives. With no explanations given by either parent, Rachelle's dad simply carried on the best he could.

No contact happened between Rachelle and her mother for several years after the airport visit that Rachelle remembered. Neither her dad nor any other family member explained any of this to the children. At the end of that several year timeframe, her mother came back and invited Rachelle to a new life in a different part of the country. Her mother went on to say she had remarried and thought Rachelle would do just fine in a new and different environment with her.

Many feelings emerged about this idea. Rachelle wanted to be with her mother, felt responsible for the younger siblings, and worried about her dad. It turned out that she did move in with her mother. Her stepdad and mother did not really get along, and a new baby added to the tension. Rachelle's mother started leaning on her a lot for moral support. That visit ended with Rachelle not feeling well on both a daily and nightly basis; she soon returned home to her dad's house. Rachelle felt there was no glue holding the family together, there were only rare emotional bonds, and everyone generally went their own way.

Once she was back with her dad, social life with her brothers and their friends became prominent. Boyfriends appeared on the scene, but something was not right in each case so she dropped each of them in turn. In her mid-teens, drugs, alcohol, and an older boyfriend created a potential risk in Rachelle's life. Her dad did not exert enough guidance and direction during this time. He just told her to go to bed when she arrived home late at night with no questions asked. As long as she did all right in school, he did not see a need for concern.

During the next summer with her mother, diet ideas caused turmoil. Rachelle felt controlling food intake equaled being in control of life. It was hard to switch back and forth between each parent. Her mother came across as controlling, right down to the choice of clothes and friends. This was not the intent. The purpose of sharing these ideas was to give guidelines on various topics and to give Rachelle a solid footing, as any good parent would do. Rachelle dressed a certain way that summer and hung out with particular friends to feel that she fit in some place in this world. Her dad was the total opposite. He did not offer enough structure or guidance. It was hard for Rachelle to feel that she fit in while at either parent's home.

Thus, began a pattern where Rachelle continued to spend high school summers with her mother and school years with her dad. There was always some amount of worry about the other parent. Siblings continued to be a concern. An internal crisis developed as a way of life. This pattern got in the way of developing a true sense of inner self that was independent from family worries.

One night, Rachelle went to a dance with her brothers and became extremely dizzy. She felt shaky and her boyfriend thought it was just a goofy stunt. One of her brothers came to her rescue the second she started to fall over. He realized something was wrong, called for help, and arranged hospital treatment. Rachelle was barely alert, just enough to wish hard to be alive and able to take a walk the next day. She prayed. Her dad had a look of panic and distress when he arrived at the hospital. Her response was extra worry about him. Over time, Rachelle and this particular brother have remained close. The two of them have talked a lot about both the good and bad aspects of their upbringing. This closeness is one of the things Rachelle leaned on in gaining a solid footing in life.

While in recovery at her dad's house, many long-buried feelings resurfaced for Rachelle that she dealt with one at a time. It was scary. She felt alone while facing worry, sadness, guilt, and even depressive feelings about the family. Her strong connection with her brother helped immensely.

Rachelle started to change and make strides in life shortly after high school graduation. Setting goals and taking responsibility became the norm. Smoking cigarettes stopped almost in one flash. Focus on health and a better future emerged shortly thereafter. During the next visit with her mother, she had high school graduation behind her and a sense of maturity underway. She stayed on, searched out employment, quit negative habits, and transformed her life. She believed that God had a hand in these changes. Rachelle worked in a couple of different schools as an instructional aide. One of the other aides took a sincere interest in her well-being, asked about her, and listened to her stories. She told Rachelle about various activities in the area, such as a library book club.

Rachelle talked about her mother once again, a reflection from years ago. Her mother seemed controlling of both Rachelle's inner and outer worlds. As a young child, Rachelle felt it was necessary to make up for being not quite all right in her mother's eyes. She believed she was to blame when her mother left the family and moved away. Later, she learned that her mother moved out for entirely different reasons.

Back to young adult life, Rachelle thought that there must be some mysterious way to get along with her mother, to feel that love. Controlling food intake to slim down seemed like a good idea at the time. That approach was like reaching for perfection, and if she worked on this, her mother would be okay with her. It became easy to overdo it. Her mother was naturally slender and food was not a concern in her own personal life. It took until Rachelle's mid to late twenties to find a balance regarding food. There were tough times until she eventually sorted it out and established a workable equilibrium.

A few years later, in a position as an educational aide, Rachelle saw children come in who reminded her of herself. They sometimes looked around as if they were a little lost, and it was such a relief to watch them settle confidently into the program. Rachelle made sure that she stood by any child she worked with. She firmly believes that even if just one person in a child's life stands by that child, it can make a huge difference. A child has to know that the adult will be there through it all, even when the child misbehaves or needs a reprimand. Once that moment is over, if the adult it still present and still loving, it can make all the difference for the child's current and future life. When this solid caring does not happen, there is a risk that the child will drift into whatever caring they can find, regardless of its form.

∞

Rachelle's way of surviving these difficult years became easier to deal with through a close relationship with one brother. She credits him with saving her life. Her spiritual journey was another important factor in the development of resilience; in addition, she made a concerted effort toward career training and advancement. At some point later in life, Rachelle took time to talk these issues over with each of her parents with forgiveness and reconciliation in mind.

Richard
"A Quest a Day"

A major turning point happened when Richard realized that he needed to switch majors in college from physics to psychology. He has worked with both younger and older students over a large number of years.

My family spoke both English and Welsh. It was a very white, Anglo-Protestant upbringing, at least until the age of twelve. We were raised in traditional nuclear families; there was not much divorce around. It gave me a strong foundation in a small community. Everybody kind of took care of each other. Some members were cool, but I didn't care for others. We played soccer as a major activity. I played soccer around age two and it was a goal of mine to become a major soccer player. I always did well academically, but my sister was much stronger than I was. I was pushed, pushed, pushed to go into sports.

At the age of sixteen, the family decided to move to the United

States. I was quite excited about it. We moved to an area outside the city, and my dad still looked for a good team for me to play on. My dad said I was a better player than he was, and he kind of lived vicariously through me in that regard. My dad's company changed and we wound up moving around... The school was so different from the first one that I thought I would attend through high school. In Britain, high school was very academic and disciplined. Here it was less formal.

There were only three or four white kids on the soccer team when I was in high school. The others were from Spain, Argentina, and other countries. In school, the population was divided between the Caucasian side and the Hispanic side. In sports, it was not that way at all. Everyone seemed to get along and was respectful of the other members. It was kind of like the Olympics in that way. Sports trumped other concerns. I did well in school here. I actually became the homecoming prince after being there for a year. I [did not] even know what it was. At first, I was... shy because of my upbringing. My sports abilities, a good demeanor, and a good personality helped me get along well and grow quite a bit.

Applying to college here was another strong learning curve experience. I was kind of on my own, but I did get some help from my sister. I got scholarships because of playing soccer. We did not have money to send me away to school, although my dad wanted to send me to college in Holland where my uncle lived, which had a professional soccer team in the area. That was my dad's plan whether I stayed in England all my life or lived here. He would have tried to send me even though we probably couldn't have afforded it. I backed out of the idea. It was just too much change for me at the time.

At first, I decided to study physics for about a year and a half. I just hated it. It wasn't that it was difficult, but it was just kind of boring. It just wasn't me; it didn't fit me at all. I also coached soccer at one of the high schools and gradually realized that my people skills were really the most helpful and natural to me. I wound up continuing to coach and actually took a group of students to Australia for about six weeks. They played over there.

I eventually took one class in psychology and found it fascinating. I started working in a children's group home. I taught the kids a lot of outdoor things like surfing and rock climbing. The salary was really low, but it did serve me well while I was finishing my undergraduate work. I knew that in psychology I needed to go beyond the bachelor's level in order to make any decent money. My visa expired while I was in Australia and when I returned here, I was given three weeks to prove that I could somehow stay in this country, or I would have to go back to England. I really loved it here. I adapted quite well. Luckily, I had the job with the group home, and they actually sponsored me with a work visa, which gave me another year to stay. The problem was that now I was applying to grad school. I found I could not afford it because I was applying as a foreign student.

What I did was go back to England, stayed there a couple of months, and applied to some graduate schools in England. I was there about six weeks and didn't have a good feeling about being back there at all. The weather, the rain, the conservative attitude, I didn't like it. Anyway, a relationship ended with a girl, so I came back to the States. I applied at the last minute and [traveled through] Mexico for about six weeks. This was my time to think about what the heck to do, and I came back in kind of a panic. I couldn't live here legally once the visa expired.

My parents helped me through my bachelor's degree, but that was as far as they could go. I found this article about green cards; it said there were going to be fifty thousand given out. Another friend and I sent in applications and his came through, and it took another week or so for mine to come through. I had applied to just one school by this time and was accepted. I went even though I didn't know how to pay for it. The green card had not come through by the time tuition was due, so I slapped it on the credit card. It was just so expensive.

When my green card came through, I applied to more schools, including some state schools. After a brief respite back in London, I found a short master's program in behavior analysis that was at least a stopgap idea while I figured out more. I then saw an article about school psychology, which sounded really interesting to me. I knew I was pretty good with kids already, plus my overall people skills were a plus. I spoke with a couple of professors who soon realized that I didn't know much about school psychology at all. One of their wives worked in that field, and I was invited to spend a day with her. I loved it right away.

I then got into the school psychology program, was focused, and really enjoyed it a lot. I lived on the campus for one year with an English roommate. It was a good experience. I finished school and completed an internship with a wonderful person in one of the school districts. There was no pay for this position, however, and I was barely surviving.

I eventually had to go back home to live, which I did for three months. I found another internship, this one was a paid position, so I moved back out, which was a big relief. This second internship was also with a wonderful person from whom I learned a lot. I'm so grateful for all of these experiences.

That school hired me and I stayed there about four years. I put in a lot of time, volunteered for extra duties, tried new things, wasn't afraid to fail, and once again I learned a lot. I didn't start out with a lot of experience in psychology, but I wasn't afraid to put myself out there and take some chances. My job experiences were so varied, in terms of people skills, and that really helped me get ahead. The rest I picked up as I went along.

It takes quite a while to get through all the education and other requirements in that field. I worked for a while in a homeless shelter in a downtown city area, plus I worked the night shift in a group home in a different city. When I look back on it, I realize how young and naïve I was. I worked with a lot of hard-core kids, gang kids, and teenage girls. I had an open mind about learning everything I could. I never felt I had to know everything, and I was lucky enough to have good people there that I really learned from. There was at least one person in every place I worked who took on the role of a mentor to some extent. I was fortunate that there were people around who would take the time to teach and not judge.

I was able to use [parts] of my background to be of some use to the kids. I'd had so many jobs and so much confusion and uncertainty at a young age. It took me a long time to come to grips with what it was I wanted to do and where I wanted to be. Without a strong family background, it would have been so much more difficult. Sometimes I could see where some of the kids were coming from. It gave me an edge in how to communicate with them and how to perhaps nudge them in the right direction. I knew that a mentor, at least one person nudging continually in a positive way, was an essential ingredient to success.

Right now, I'm working on building my life with good people around me. You know how life changes so quickly. You can be on top of the world one minute and have a disaster happen the next. I've been lucky that I haven't had major losses or major trauma in my life... relative; I guess it's all relative... There were some times when I might not have been able to cope with certain issues, but I did cope with those that I had to deal with. I was lucky to have a support system. Even in relationships, people need to remember to talk to each other, go back, and apologize when that's in order. It takes strength to make relationships strong. I'm looking forward to having kids; I'll try open dialogue with them. Parents blunder in that. They've got to show the human side of themselves. We'll see what happens. My family taught us to always have a backup plan when we do things, to live by the law "the right way, squared away."

Moving from one country to another challenges just about anyone's life. Richard had a strong family support system in his early years; he had at least one mentor at every major undertaking along the way in his later education and career experiences. Families and mentors often play a major role in the development of resilience in an individual's life. This support system helped Richard find the strength to solve problems and learn to make wise decisions.

Nanette
"Just Go for It!"

Nanette maintained an upbeat and positive attitude throughout her ordeal with cancer. She definitely provided a role model for those in contact with her during those years. Her career involved administrative duties in a program that dealt with younger and older children.

Nanette saw herself as naturally resilient; she was not prone to worry or get upset about what might happen. Distinguishing between things in her control and those things out of her control came easy. Self-esteem, even as a child, was on the plus side. Her mother added to Nanette's confidence at an early age by providing positive comments about her abilities. She maintained a go-for-it attitude, which led to emphasizing upbringing as key to resilience, while some friends thought resilience was strictly innate.

Nanette's own resilience underwent a severe trial after surgery. Too many relatives were right there—it was stunning to see them. Something was terribly wrong. Surgery had been urgent but not life threatening. Nanette woke up to learn that she had severe cancer that was almost everywhere in her body.

Cancer never crossed her mind in the past, yet here it was. In just a flash, her life changed. The next few weeks were nightmarish with surgeries, the start of treatment, and then even more surgeries; it went on like this for a while. Treatments seemed to last forever, especially when additional medications became necessary as new situations developed. Parts of Nanette's body felt cold, while other parts felt tingly at times.

It helped to count down—one therapy session done, X more to go. It was easier to live with that way. Sometimes, it took willpower to make it all right to go through certain types of sickness, especially nausea, because treatments that started with nausea were actually therapy in the larger scheme of things. This larger scheme included an ability to walk, which remained important at all times. Walking became difficult, but Nanette could still do it, and she was grateful for that. She kept a renewed focus on that big picture. One difficult decision was to back out of certain professional aspects of work life. It was fun being on the go and doing things. It was difficult for her to think about slowing down her schedule, let alone backing out of prior work commitments. Nonetheless, a highly modified plan emerged. Nanette's reading time could increase. A plan was developed among coworkers to email back and forth regarding a variety of topics; this felt good to everyone.

With an upbeat, optimistic attitude throughout life, Nanette took the glass half-full approach. Spiritual life did not waver during this period. Once back on solid footing, a new routine developed.

A short walk came first and then it gradually built up as much as possible. During time away from work, Nanette learned to appreciate walks through a local park again. It helped bring her back to nature, and simple things became enjoyable, such as feeding the ducks.

Prior to this time in life, Nanette concentrated largely on work and lived on the fast track. It was common to race home from work, do errands, take a class at the gym, and then go out to dinner. Even on vacation, work went with her. Home life became more important now because it existed in abundance; this approach reflects sound mental health. Reading time did increase and she taught herself several arts and crafts activities. Her workbench in the garage finally saw some good use.

When Nanette first had to be home a lot, she deliberately chose hobbies and activities that meshed with being home. This led to thorough enjoyment with many of these new endeavors. Even when she was further along in recovery, she often chose to stay in on weekends and work on projects. Nanette became better acquainted with herself this way instead of keeping super busy or socializing as she did in the past. This change caused Nanette to study about introversion and extroversion. Some friends of hers are extroverts, so they are always ready to be with others; they recharge by having company. Other friends are introverts, and they recharge by being alone. It has been interesting for Nanette to find a new balance with these friends, as well as a new balance for herself.

When first back at work, Nanette got sick after only a week, even a few hours a day put her at risk. She recovered quickly, but she remembered the doctor's comment on how cancer and low white blood cells go together. About a month following her return to good health, Nanette made a flight reservation and the date was coming up soon. It was just for a short trip, but it would involve a crowded plane; a question came up about going at all and about the wisdom of wearing a mask. Her confidence was high about getting stronger day by day; she expected to take this trip and be just fine.

Cancer changes more than just the individual patient; your family changes at the same time. Her children worried, especially once they realized their dad, her ex, would be away on a trip for a while. The extended family called and visited more routinely. Everyone kept in touch by phone.

Nanette revealed something personal. She would rather not have had cancer ever, let alone all the treatment, but if it were required, it would be best just to go for it. This was her typical response to challenges. Life happens; you just have to take it on.

Now that Nanette is back working full time, her attitude is that when a workday ends no work goes home at all and extra tasks have to wait. Starting in mid-afternoon, coworkers stop by to say good night!

Life was on the fast track in Nanette's past. Zooming through gym equipment and pressing herself to 'last longer' on particular machines was a normal routine. Her energy level allowed that before cancer treatments started. Once treatment was underway enough to allow any kind of return to the gym, she felt lucky to last two minutes. One to three miles at a time is now a common walking distance; it is equally common to switch among walk days, gym days, and rest days. Treadmills are not as much fun as the rose garden! Yoga and other indoor classes come in handy during winter months. Nanette mentioned that old saying about having to slow down whether you want to or not. She joked that in this case, it was more than a slowdown; it was more like a sudden stop! Doctors made a big impression on her about balance. It is healthy to have activities, and it is important not to 'catch' something.

Nanette talked about how eating habits have changed, along with most things in life. Weight came off during the hospital stay, as food was undesirable that whole time. Her appetite was way off. Once home, a meal consisted of a spoonful of soup and two slices of apple for starters. All flavors of various brands of ice cream remained familiar! Nanette ate better when she really forced herself. It was essential, so she did it. A necessarily strong push in that direction lasted quite a while. Doctors reminded her to eat from the four food groups each meal, so she ate very small amounts frequently throughout the day. Family members prepared food ahead, which made a huge difference. Casseroles, meatloaf, poultry, and fish dishes, along with an array of soft desserts and lots of ice cream, topped it all off to absolute perfection. These items went into Nanette's freezer and lasted for months.

Her hair started falling out due to treatment; once she got past the initial shock, she made a decision that it was not worth crisis energy. There are hats, scarves, headbands, and wigs to help. Spiritual life proved helpful throughout this time; church attendance was useful. Everything necessary would happen just as it should. Her part in the job was to work hard, save up, look forward, and take steps toward the future. Her attitude was it would all work out.

Self-care was important and there was absolute confidence that she would have any care she needed. In her mind's eye, that connects to religion. Her life has been one of self-assurance, exertion, and success. If she should die sooner rather than later, that would simply be the way it was. Many aspects of everyday life had been hers to enjoy thoroughly over the years. This included marriage, family, travel, friends, education, and a good living environment. She has had it all, done it all, and feels lucky to be alive to say so.

A trip to Paris was in the works. Her family was from Europe and plenty of family and friends still lived there. This plan was wildly different from prior experiences. Trips used to involve running around to each place and sometimes back again. This time, there was no pressure to visit people or places. The plan was to let the others know when and where she would be. If they came by to spend time together, that would be nice. Visits to cities or other areas may occur during this visit, if she felt up to it. Her interests were endless, but she became choosier about how to spend energy.

One example of resilience was in Nanette's willingness to develop new hobbies, the kind a person could work on at home. She made this choice when it became apparent that the fast track, all day and half the night, no longer worked. If something did not work the way it used to, then Nanette was determined to find some way around it. This resilience feature led to wise choices regarding exercise, work, recreation, and visits with family and friends. Her mom's attitude and teachings during Nanette's childhood years certainly reflected resilience as well.

Beth
"Explore, Investigate, and Then Proceed"

Through trial and error, Beth learned about setting and maintaining boundaries. She learned to honor approaches to life that suited her best. She was a travel agent and business owner for many years. At times, she was also involved in the education field.

Beth realized after graduating high school that she had two choices. One was to please her parents, while another was to do things to achieve a promising and satisfactory life. She did not understand the outside world very well. Life up to this point included lots of church time, especially on Sundays. That religious background came with a lot of stress and guilt about right and wrong behaviors. There was so much more to learn about functioning in the real world than she ever imagined. At around age eighteen, Beth was barely equipped to live in a nunnery.

Although her parents were not fanatics about many aspects of their church, they were strict concerning ideas of sin. Beth asked permission to go bowling with high school friends; her mother threw that request right back at her. Her mother said Beth would not have asked, except she knew that to go bowling was a sin. This flew in the face of how Beth grew up; permission was normal and required to attend events. Guilt was what Beth got out of that encounter. She did not go bowling, and she did not get an answer from her mother.

Plenty of boyfriends came around but because they were not churchgoers, they were not welcomed. Beth's mother took the lead at home, and her dad went along on most issues. They tolerated a somewhat older man who came around because he attended church. He and Beth made an agreement that marriage would occur several years later, so she gave him money and they bought several acres of land.

Beth's fiancé became quite ill; after the checkup was complete and tests were underway, the doctor asked them to return in a few weeks. After that elapsed time, they learned that Beth's fiancé had a serious illness that required complicated treatment and surgery. In the meantime, her fiancé made additional land purchases using money in their joint account. The treatment and surgeries soon followed. Depression became a high risk for him.

While at the apartment collecting certain envelopes and files for her fiancé, Beth saw an envelope addressed 'to whom it may concern.' Thinking this meant her, she opened it. The will and financial information inside mentioned other people but not Beth. While at the bank to straighten this out, the manager explained that there was no signature card with her name on it for the account. Her fiancé turned in other cards but not hers. What was the full story here? A question about what became of her money quickly developed into a panicky thought.

When Beth picked up her fiancé's sister to go to the hospital, she had no idea if this sister actually knew about his actions. Confusion reigned about how to proceed; a minister agreed to hold a copy of the will and act as Beth's witness. Her fiancé died shortly thereafter. Due to trust in this man, Beth lost all her money. She could not live with her parents' ideas any longer, not as she had in the past.

Beth moved to a new city and worked as an accountant. For her mom, this move must have been as jarring as a huge earthquake. Beth met her future husband in this city; he traveled a lot for work and did well in his field. Once their second child was born, Beth realized that something was way off track, but she stayed in the marriage due to obligation and pressure. Beth again mentioned her parents; they did nothing to teach her about living in the world and making wise decisions. She had to learn those things over time; they included painful lessons.

When Beth and her husband divorced, she explained to the children that living with her or living with their dad would be two very different things. He could provide in ways she had no means to do. His accounts were out of reach. Once settled in, they could come over for a visit. Much to her surprise, they were on the porch upon her arrival. Some things clicked and started to fall into place; a career path developed that was inspired by the travel she and her husband did because of his work. He was high up in his company; his contacts became her friends and acquaintances. She thought of first working in and then opening a travel agency;

travel experience, plus business studies at a local university, inspired Beth's confidence regarding this type of endeavor.

Beth described this educational pursuit as a type of rebirth. Her focus was on how to raise the children well and how to develop this career to support them. Thinking about losses, disappointments, and confusion stopped. Her ex-husband often called to invite their children to move back in with him; sometimes these offers included travel jaunts. The children did keep in touch with their dad, but they mainly lived with their mom. Beth's parents supported a continuation of the marriage, which was unhelpful. There was a lot to endure with the divorce alone; Beth did manage to function at work and keep her job, though it was difficult at times. She wondered how much more was necessary to learn about relationships and living in the world; some trust slowly emerged regarding future decisions. She maintained a graceful way about herself, and she had a positive attitude about life.

Upcoming 'deals' were talked about by her ex whenever he called Beth to discuss money. He often chatted with the children, which she supported. Any extra money was for them, not for her. Actually, the last day her ex ever worked was before they divorced. He managed to live off their savings all that time. Other than child support money, Beth did not have anything to do with her ex-husband. She learned more about his underhandedness as time went on. Although Beth learned from parents and church about the importance of having a husband, she said that on the inside she learned that it was not necessary to have a husband or a wife for a good life.

The idea of owning a business enterprise grew stronger for Beth each year. With a friend's help, Beth became the owner of a travel agency and eventually hired additional agents. Her ability to pay back loans sooner than expected was due to hard work and the forward-looking attitude she and her boys maintained about the business. This friend credited Beth for both the discipline and knowledge of travel agency work. Beth reflected that these years involved the most intense work of her whole life.

She took responsibility for her part in various situations she described, and she chalked it up to how much time it took to learn about some of the practical sides of life. During years in the travel business, she developed internal strength. Doors opened and a sixth sense emerged about a variety of topics. Beth shared experiences and quandaries with some of the wide variety of people now in her life; these conversations contributed to mutual problem solving and success.

Her parents' focus on the negatives gave Beth something to ponder. This approach did not encourage curiosity or initiative. She teaches family members, including her grandchildren, about both positives and negatives, whether regarding a decision, an adventure, a challenge, a problem, or a potential opportunity they face.

Beth showed resilience through coping with situations, even when changing course proved difficult. She provided resources for her children and grandchildren that will serve them well. These include curiosity, investigation, and taking deliberate actions, which are all parts of resilience.

Carol
"Long Ago"

Carol expressed enthusiasm for each of her children's adventures in life. She maintained that upbeat approach even when her children came home with wild ideas. One example is when the quieter child came home and announced he was planning to be the star of the school play!

Carol began by talking about before and after therapy in her life. For years, she was perfectly happy and life was just dandy. Something almost unconscious bothered her, though, which simply did not quit. She wished there had been a stronger tie with her mother, and she wished her father had been more involved in her activities throughout her childhood. She secretly worried that maybe their drinking habits went beyond cocktail hour rituals.

Therapy started just as her life was on a spiral and heading out of control. One big therapy issue was how scary her dad was at times. Some of that was all right; some of it was creepy. Carol learned to cope, to fit in, and was in a quandary many times. If the ability to redo her past existed, the next issue would be for her mom and Carol to have been closer than they were. Emotional closeness was hard to come by. Maybe this was because her mom was simply not available in that way. Confiding at all was rare. During family trips and on the many outings they shared, Carol often felt lonely. At the same time, she enjoyed participation in every imaginable child's activity, from dance class wearing tap shoes to art class making clay designs. Her mom was involved in a variety of arts and crafts activities, so those mutual interests provided some closeness.

During earlier years, Carol remembered family events with pleasure. Over the past year or two, though, she remembered more negatives than positives. Through therapy, Carol hoped to learn how to let go of some things and enjoy memories of other things. Many outings, driving trips, and camping trips were fun-filled events for the whole family. It would be fun to enjoy those memories again.

There were often uncomfortable moments in Carol's childhood when her dad was around. Her brother and mother seemed oblivious to any danger signs. They regarded him as just boisterous and rowdy. Partly due to his large size, Carol thought of him as too touchy-feely scary at times. At other times, of course, he was a huge comfort to the entire family. Carol often dismissed any bad feelings. Putting on a brave face and using extroversion skills helped, as well as ignoring inside conflicts as much as possible. Depressive moments, questions about self-esteem, and insecurities with action and activities were hidden beneath the surface.

In adulthood, Carol was determined that she and her mom should connect more, and her dad should follow the limits she set in her own household. For one thing, smoking was restricted to outdoors only. Carol's husband and an aunt, the guardian angel type, worked hard in their talks with her to be realistic about what she could really change. They did not think Carol's parents were willing or able to make changes. There were difficult moments about all this, and there were trials and errors over many visits back and forth. In the end, Carol turned to a therapist to come to grips with it all and move forward in life. At that beginning point, therapy was a difficult process; it was kind of like jumping into an ice-cold pool and then realizing you had to swim all the way across whether you like it or not. Family support from both her husband and aunt helped a lot; Carol's children continued to share their normal activities with her. She got through it by gritting her teeth most of the time.

Progress was rapid in Carol's life at this point. She started to let go of what was not going to change. Throughout life, she was strong in setting aside some things in order to accomplish other things. Even in those depressive moments, attending her children's school activities remained a priority. Gradually, healing deep inside did happen. This was a years-long process. Her husband is the main person who knows all she went through to reach that healing point. The therapist and some close girlfriends know many stories; Carol feels proud of her accomplishment. She is proud that she chose the direction of hard work and did not fall apart and let her life slide by unattended.

Carol thought about ending everything; some days the negatives far outweighed the positives. One more step seemed like just too much at various times during her process. At those moments, only despair, depression, hopelessness, and worse things were visible. She could not always see light at the end of the tunnel...but one more step...one talk with someone...and she found sure footing again. Carol wanted to tell the reader that if they could just get through that point and get past it, it could prove to be their best move.

Life today far exceeds anything Carol even hoped for back then. Such harmony and contentment are far beyond her wildest dreams. Carol's confidence and self-esteem are way up; this helps her children build their own confidence. They watch their mom do better and better, which in turn reinforces their best in behavior and choices.

Her relationship with her husband has gotten even better throughout their history together. It was good and now it is far better than anything she could have imagined. He has made some changes of his own, which he did for her in the beginning; these changes have helped him in his own life too.

One of Carol's main points of pride is to be on a different path from the one her parents took. She did not repeat their patterns. She listens to her children and maintains an emotional bond, and she is conscious of teaching boundaries and individual responsibility. This is a positive approach to take with the children, while she, in turn, receives immense personal satisfaction from living this way.

Even with these advances, there are still times when she slips back into confusion, unfulfilled wishes, and is just plain out of balance. Talk radio programs or TV commercials often form a trigger. Carol is sad about her parents' lack of communication with her; she still hopes that will change. This lack of communication is an unpleasant fact, but it is not something that keeps her up at night. She prefers and strives to live every day in the present tense.

Therapy gave her a toolbox plus an instruction manual that was worth going over page by page. With therapy finished, the office phone number stayed in that toolbox just in case an occasional reminder about something or other would prove beneficial down the road. With the toolbox at her disposal, Carol could face the world confidently and move forward. She mentioned that old saying about standing up and dusting yourself off when you fall down, and she added that punching as she came up might be required. It is still easier for her to stick up for someone else than for herself at times, but she is learning how to do that.

Compassion and gentleness, combined with strength, is Carol's way of describing herself. There is contentment in looking ahead and not back. Certain aspects of childhood were not what she wished for; in contrast, her current family life is close to ideal. She confirmed that she has 'everything' already and she can live without 'more.' To become insatiable would not serve her well.

Carol talked a little about generosity and the more spiritual side of life. When one is generous in some way, more comes back, either in the same way or in an entirely different way. She mentioned God and awareness; when she has fallen short of her best, she just gets going again and carries on. She makes fresh starts as often as necessary and focuses on improvement.

One person in Carol's life as a youngster was a close aunt. At a young age, this person made all the difference, and help from at least one person is a common theme in developing resilience. Through support from her aunt and her husband, coupled with a developing belief in her own abilities, Carol gained the strength to overcome obstacles, set realistic goals, and make wise decisions.

Diane
"A Too-Perfect Picture of Perfection"

Diane established and renewed boundaries once she realized the problems she and her husband had to face regarding their wish for a family. She worked as a receptionist/scheduler/organizer in a local medical practice.

As a young adult, Diane felt a lot of pressure, some of it probably from her mom, to marry and carry on in life from that position. She dated a large number of people, and as time went on, Diane found fewer people around who she would ever consider for marriage. Mental baggage was not something tolerable. She was fussy about who she dated right from the start. One example was a bias against the sloppy look that was popular at the time. If someone owned an expensive car but was untidy in how they dressed, Diane was not interested.

People arrived at the office with long stories about one thing or another; her thought was "No, she did not want to live that way." She owned a condominium, furniture, appliances, nice clothes, and all the fixings. With education under her belt, she took care of her health, worked out at a gym, and lived a down-to-earth, simple, and productive life.

Diane matured early, set out to accomplish goals, and did so with relative ease. There was no reliance on finding a husband, which certain family members would have preferred. She checked many of life's goals off her list before even meeting her husband. When they did meet, Diane found him to be a sweet and caring person, which continues through to the present day. This is true even with an upbringing that left them wondering about his family and confused him at times.

Spiritual life is even more valuable now than it was during her college years. It was unnecessary throughout college, even though it was a solid part of her earlier life. Her parents shared their religious understanding with their children; they put no expectation on what any of them would decide about it all once they became adults.

Friends told Diane that her apartment looked like that of a married woman. All of this was well before she made any wedding plans. They were surprised at the amount of food she had on hand. She humorously told them that she ate meals, so she kept food on hand. They thought single people ate out, heated TV dinners, or ate peanut butter and jelly sandwiches. There was no concept whatsoever of Diane's life where you leave home and live as a truly independent adult on your own. Her mother taught Diane and her siblings that marriage does not make them important, that being human does.

Diane's hair was close to perfect at all times. It was important even while she was a youngster; her sister fixed it for her. Life continued under Diane's control in all kinds of ways; this included exercise, her current position, looks, and her lifestyle, among others. She had no idea how to handle the stress that came next. It seemed next to impossible for Diane and her husband to conceive when that desired time came into their lives. She had grown up making goals and accomplishing them. How could something like having a baby become so completely out of her control? Her immediate answer was fate, luck, or God's hand.

Diane's way of processing, however important in details, did not treat these issues as one extreme or another. Not having children would not make them bad people. In normal life, it goes both ways—some people had children and others did not; there was no judgment either way. This attitude saved them from having worst-case responses. It took time to get through it all, but Diane avoided serious depression by realizing that although they wanted a child, it looked like it was simply not a part of their future. The disappointment was enormous, but they would get through it. This did not stop Diane and her husband from medical and other explorations, which she discussed later in this story.

She jumped to a topic of nieces and nephews and fantasized for a moment about how they would remember her in years to come. Perhaps they would bring a sweater to her at a future home where older folks live. They might remember those birthday gift cards from years ago. A person's own children might remember things differently; these memories might be closer to their heart, although sometimes children and parents do not connect at all. You have to want to raise children and not have them just so they can take care of you later.

Nothing Diane and her husband tried worked; neither doctors' offices nor specialized clinics in the area could help them achieve their desired results. At times, they paused long enough to ask themselves how much money and energy should go in this direction. One thought was to move onto other topics; they joked about world cruises, buying a mansion, and climbing a snowy mountaintop.

They were not through yet. Talks then came with lawyers concerning adoption, which stopped them in their tracks again due to the costs involved. Did they really want to go through with that idea? With each visit came more worry and concern;

vulnerability issues drained their energy. Even the lawyers told them that sometimes what looks promising falls through. This happens because the birth mother changes her mind or feels the connection with the adoptive parents is not acceptable.

Their next stop was with human services people. Diane and her husband wondered if there would be a foster-adopt situation that might work. Children in need at that time came from backgrounds that included drugs, alcohol, and a myriad of other issues. Diane felt that adequate parenting in those cases was not something either of them could adequately provide. Their stamina and temperaments did not fit those needs. She read about these children and heard from a couple of friends that sometimes children in these cases have trouble accepting that they belong and fit in at all with anyone, anywhere. Sometimes problems persist through the years. Diane and her husband were what they considered somewhat older already; their hesitancy caused them to turn down this opportunity. They give a lot of credit to people who can capably contribute in that way. It was not for them.

They decided to forget pregnancy as an idea altogether. Nothing about pressing forward toward wanting and having a baby made sense any more. It was time to regroup and go in other directions. The next thing Diane knew she was pregnant. This was extremely unexpected after all medical interventions failed. Adoption went out of the picture and Diane started picturing herself in maternity clothes. Nausea did not put a damper on how wonderful she felt! Just as unexpectedly, one day several weeks later, the embryo's heartbeat stopped. That stopped just about everything in Diane and her husband's lives. The heartbeat came and went, started and then stopped. Blame did not fit in anywhere. That part of life simply and completely ended.

Enough already. It was time to move on; it was time to create a different environment. Remodeling the house came next—inside and out, top to bottom. They cleaned out and gave away many things, and they redid ceilings, floors, and the fireplace. This helped them clear out their own inside issues, in addition to making household improvements.

Diane received a call from a family friend two or three months later. This friend knew of a birth mom looking for adoptive parents. Diane's first response was to say just forget it, but she did agree to take the call. From lawyers during prior meetings, Diane had heard nightmare stories about the difficulties of even talking with a birth mom, let alone hearing nitty-gritty details about pregnancy, health of the baby, and so on. This birth mom talked with Diane right away and eagerly shared how the baby had progressed so far, and she talked about doctor's comments, etc., quite openly. Diane and her husband adopted this perfectly healthy baby and maintained a certain amount of contact with the birth mom. The birth mom invited Diane to the delivery room. Diane's husband arranged, via a doctor's visit, for a time when the birth mom could see the baby.

It haunted Diane when she realized she had come full circle. She was part of a picture-perfect family from years past, and she was part of a picture-perfect family now with baby in tow. She, her husband, and the birth mom maintain some contact; Diane sent photos, and the birth mom called to wish them a Happy New Year.

Family support is a key to developing resilience needed throughout life; it helps in facing every obstacle and in making wise decisions. In Diane's case, her mother was instrumental in teaching her own children the importance of independence in thought and action. She gave them a strong foundation with basic structure.

Melissa
"One Step at a Time"

Melissa was a competent, friendly business owner of a highly successful restaurant. At that time, most of her children were an active part of the business, and they often had repeat customers.

Melissa and her husband had several children; he was handy around the house. She stayed highly engaged with her children's activities, and they kept as busy as ever. Then her husband dropped dead. She described herself as highly introverted, which she translated into not having an identity, especially in the years prior to marriage. For continued family contact on her husband's side, she and the children moved to another part of the country where her husband's brother lived. It turned out, however, that he was in no position to spend time with them. They found themselves on their own.

Melissa went to a doctor in order to cope with the situation of being a young widow with several young children, living in a new state, and figuring out how to support a family. The doctor prescribed meds. There seemed to be one for each mood, but there was no support to see a counselor. Melissa eventually told the doctor that she was no longer taking any meds. When he heard that, he started talking about hospitals and orphanages.

Melissa threw the meds out, quit that doctor, found a counselor, and began a new life. It was quite appalling that the doctor, that any doctor, would behave like that. She settled in quite well with the new counselor. Melissa talked and the counselor listened. Once she started hearing out loud what was running through her mind, it started to become clear; gradually things started falling into place. Melissa knew, at a gut level, that running a restaurant would fit with her interests and abilities, even though there would be so much to learn at first. It was important to learn how to talk with other people, especially as an introvert. Everything she learned was at an intellectual level at first; it took quite a few years to get it to register on inside levels.

Even though Melissa felt good after the counseling, there was a lot of work to do to get a new self from head to heart; those inside levels house emotions and deep belief. She often felt shaky about who she was; her insides and identity were not solid yet. It took a tremendous amount of processing. One friend invited Melissa to lunch at Melissa's own restaurant. Now was the moment to admit who the owner actually was! No mention of the restaurant had occurred before then. Enough was enough; the weird feelings going back and forth about even opening a restaurant had come to a stop. It was now time to accept herself, her abilities, and these accomplishments, at another level altogether.

Certain invitations for visits that were automatic while her husband was alive suddenly changed dramatically. It felt like discrimination. Even when visiting people her family often visited, she sensed a big difference the whole time. It did not matter that sometimes these invitations were from close family members. She chalked it up partly to being a widowed mom with young children and partly to the need to let her personal identity re-emerge. There was a need to become more comfortable within herself, as herself.

Many feelings required acknowledgment, sorting out, then letting go, regardless of how strong or negative they were. It was like having to swim all the way across the pool to be free again. Once at the other side, Melissa could step out and away from all that distress. This provided a rebirth of sorts. The process was time consuming, and usually contained obstacles, but it worked because she pushed forward, even when it sometimes required repeated steps. It is a good idea to put an idea or a picture of your best possible self in your mind and then practice every day to get there. Melissa did as much growing up as her children did over these years, which contributed to the large amount of talking and understanding among these close family members.

Her therapist got credit for helping Melissa identify strengths and abilities. Specifics emerged about developing a productive, thriving life. Strength in math would be a big help in a business enterprise. She had been taking all sorts of classes, only some of which were her strong suit. It finally became clear which direction she should go in for success; the restaurant opened shortly thereafter. As the restaurant business continued, Melissa's math skills came in handy for expenses, taxes, and financial goals; it was easy to think about correct decisions ahead of time. Not every cent needed to be calculated all summer long to know how to get through the slower winter season.

Her attitude has changed over time. Earlier, Melissa thought she needed a caretaker of sorts. This was not true. She was fully capable of guiding herself on many levels, and she had been doing so all along. In her earlier years, no one was available to care for her, to provide support. The problem was that of feeling half-empty for many years without realizing it. After her husband's death, offers of help poured in, though it was a different kind of help from what she sought. Her idea of help was to learn to find her own answers and to grow from within, to gain what she now calls her identity. This was not forthcoming. Friends and relatives wanted to help her the way they wanted to help, not how she wanted their help.

In social arenas, men sometimes like a woman to be, or at least to act, weaker. When a woman spoke up strongly, it provoked questions. There were a couple of narrow escapes; some people did not encourage Melissa's personal growth and independent thought.

She was grateful to see through these encounters well enough in advance to save herself from potential bad situations and decisions.

Melissa declared the world better get out of her way once her mind is clear about an idea. Strength comes from way inside after mulling ideas over and contemplating how they might work out. Ideas play around in her mind's eye. Occasionally, Melissa shares a bit with others, seeks feedback at times, and may keep an idea or two. Sometimes feedback makes her doubt herself, or at best, pushes her to rethink an approach.

Then one day, Melissa flings off that protective shell and continues with her mind fully made up. She acknowledges and accepts this pattern about life, and she has fun with it. This idea contrasts with that of some of her friends. They proceed like a tornado or a racecar with quick moves and quick jumps to their own successes.

It became important to learn more about that good feeling of decision-making and confidence, because it comes, goes, and slips away at times. These up and down moments are a part of life; they are not a permanent backslide. It is best not to dwell on them; instead, take the next step to get to the present and move forward.

Sometimes a customer or friend that she has not seen in ages will stop by to say hello. They comment that she always looks the same; it looks like nothing has changed. She chuckles with them, and they have an enjoyable visit. Later, Melissa will think about changes that have happened in her life, especially on the inside. Even the kids do not know every new thing about her. She is mainly the mom who runs the business, bakes brownies at home, and cares about them.

Melissa watched her children develop over the years. She was grateful they continued to do well in school, stayed away from drugs and alcohol, and developed into strong people. They know about hard work, as they take turns opening the restaurant each morning!

Melissa's comment about working hard for something you want rings true for many people. Grit and perseverance got her through her husband's death, raising children, and opening the restaurant. Although it was a long road, she kept plugging away without fail. Regardless of obstacles along the way, Melissa found inner confidence to stick up for ideas and to achieve goals. She charted a new path for her life and her children's lives, which provided a strong example of resilience for them now and into their futures.

Tim
"If You Would Listen Just Once"

Travel provided one turning point for Tim. Another turning point was his abrupt job change away from one field and toward another. He worked in the field of education for many years.

In elementary school, Tim had the best of everything to start with—grades, no trouble, and was generally a good kid. Intuitively, he wondered what else there was to offer; was there a talent or gift? No one showed any interest in that topic. How to bring this subject up to adults around him remained a dilemma. How could he fit in, what about adulthood? Tim already fit in better than most with his grades and behaviors. Before high school, he was also the best in athletics and the most popular.

Those accolades had no meaning for him; it was just luck. It all seemed shallow and unsatisfying. This unspoken hurdle—a question about talent and gifts—deep inside where no one else saw, stayed there a long time. School was always fine; his mom was an educator, and he liked school and learning to start with. He never truly became a student regardless of his high grades. Tim never really studied, which he considered a bad thing years later.

Peer groups became important in high school. This caused Tim to get lower grades on purpose. They went down from "A" grades to "B" or "C" grades in an effort to change his peer group. His desire for belonging became intense. Having that belonging goal might be similar to how gang members feel at times. Even with already belonging to the right crowds in someone's view, Tim was not satisfied. This was a huge turning point in his life. Through high school, his grades remained just average to somewhat above average.

More average in various ways now, flowing with the tide, not the best, still wondering where to go from here, what to do in life as an adult, were his daily quandaries. No one paid attention; no one really asked Tim inside questions. This was as true with high grades as it was with average performance. Students today, too, often get that same treatment, with no questions asked and no inquiries made. Life went on that way.

Tim's grades dropped and this made his parents unhappy. Over the next few months, they hardly communicated at all. His parents believed that you must follow rules, but they maintained a tolerant attitude. Rules were easy enough to follow, especially for a good kid. This was his rebellious stage. He ditched school a couple of times and wound up in juvenile custody once. A part of that custody experience follows.

Tim's time in juvenile custody matched his behavior at that time. He was the one person not drinking at the party. He was both like the others and not like the others because of his decision not to drink. Everyone else jumped out the windows as soon as the police showed up. Tim stayed put. No one got away; they all landed in juvenile custody. Even with his comment to the police that he did not drink alcohol, he received rough treatment, handcuffs included, right along with the rest. His dad had one comment for him at the pickup office. This was the 'one and only time' his dad would ever pick him up from juvenile detention. If it happened again, he would have to stay. Tim described this as a blend of his parents' idea of following rules and showing tolerance at the same time.

This occurred during Tim's early teen years. It was rebellious but also like taking a step leading toward independence. His parents tolerated the situation, which Tim wondered about ever being able to do as a parent himself. No drama occurred at home; Tim probably went to his room while his parents were confused and disappointed. This type of scene never happened again.

Tim switched topics in this talk back to school and studies. Teachers and parents instructed him to study, but that never happened, not even for big tests. Study habits were not his thing; there was no memory of actually handing in schoolwork, though it was required. Even getting through his dissertation, which did take some work, never pained him as it did his friends. He completed schoolwork without passion but with a level of annoyance. This was also his approach to studies right through college.

Life changed again at that point when the opportunity to travel suddenly and unexpectedly emerged. Trip plans became solid and soon the means developed to travel the world rather than visit just one or two countries. Two main lessons occurred during this travel time. The discovery of talent was one. Tim's talent was in wanting to help people, and helping others was something he could do and do well. This led to Tim investigating social work as his future.

Having confidence in himself and his ability to survive anywhere was the second thing that extensive travel taught him.

This experience of travel, and the mixed cultures of over fifty countries, paved the way for that confidence to take hold. Tim's parents told him years before that he could do anything that he put his mind to. Successful travel reinforced that idea. Tim sensed limitations, which might have been fear or reluctance within him, but all that seemed to disappear. Once a social worker position got underway, it became obvious that this was not his route toward helping others. What he saw instead, in that specific work environment, was a fostering of too much dependence. What he wanted was to find a way to help others discover and use their own abilities toward growth and independence.

His next idea was to look into teaching. His mom taught him a lot about that field, his own school experience was solid, and he earned a teaching credential as part of his journey. Tim's first teaching assignment was perfect. He worked with strong students and became a coach, all while in an environment of younger educators. The principal saw other talent in him. He realized that Tim could work with struggling students as well as strong ones, so he asked him to take over a class with students who needed extra support. Tim's first response was to remain as coach; he was good for the students currently assigned to him. The principal, far-sighted and imaginative, could see other possibilities. Tim and the principal got along well; eventually, Tim agreed to try a change of positions. This proved to be the beginning of the end, or maybe the end of the beginning.

Students thrown out of other classes came Tim's way; his connection with these students was immediate. Staff trusted him due to their experience with him as a varsity coach; he used his stature to talk with each teacher about how things might improve and what would work for a second chance. A solid connection with students helped him understand that they were good students and had contributions to make.

Both strong abilities and areas of trouble came clearly into view. Once these students and Tim learned to talk together about the related issues and face the confusing and contradictory parts, they were more at ease in establishing a solid footing in life. This experience totally reinforced Tim's idea that students need adults to talk with them and listen to them. Students have a lot inside and often need help in creating a clear direction for growth.

Full circle is one way of describing this experience. Recognition and mentoring are two of the most important factors of education. Exposure to different arenas of possibility, and sometimes a push to explore more in a certain direction, means a lot to some students. Tim's passion for these topics continued. He also cared about students who otherwise felt ignored at school and at home. Ignored is exactly how he felt years ago. Plenty of students feel pushed away by society. The program that Tim developed stresses contact with each student. Another time he found himself in a position to influence many educators and did so through workshops, speakers, and small group sessions, as well as by individual chats.

The best way to go forth is to have each classroom build a community. This generates help for each student and provides support for any educator. Once Tim built a community with students in the classroom, a solid foundation for success flourished. The first students he worked with were ones mentioned earlier; they attended a school with a visionary principal who understood Tim right from the start. Students settled into classroom life; newcomers learned the ropes right away. Discipline was not an issue. His base group of students stayed with him for a solid year. It would have been difficult to accomplish this goal about community if students came and went quickly.

Tim believes that today's students will solve tomorrow's

problems. Every generation has problems; many solutions develop later. A natural evolution of ideas and stories go right along with our lines of genetic information. There are no free rides; everyone has a purpose or some contribution to make. The lucky ones are those who latch onto something and go for it. It does not matter how small or large it is, focusing on one task at a time works. This is what happened in Tim's life, and it is something for which he is especially grateful. It is kind of like an answer to questions from back in those teen years. As a search-oriented person, he keeps his eyes open to the future. Tim is confident and focused; he encourages others to push ahead, to push their envelopes, and to see what emerges.

Even at a young age, Tim realized that his dad had developed a good balance between enforcing structure and letting go. He used this balance to develop his own balance. Extensive travel, coupled with that early family support, taught Tim many resilience skills that he needed to make sound choices. Once Tim and his colleagues found educational tools to help students initiate a positive life plan and develop their own resilience, he encouraged their use in every possible way.

CONCLUSION

Writing this book has been quite the journey. It lasted a lot longer than I first anticipated for a variety of reasons. It seemed to take forever to transcribe the recorded stories. At first, the length of the stories and the number of themes were just fine. That was before I met my first editor. After I received input from several editors early on, I learned that it was important to cut back on the number of children's stories in order to avoid repetition. It was equally important to shorten each of the adult stories. The best way to do that was to reread each story carefully enough to pick out the storyteller's themes. Setting a maximum of two themes per story worked, and in most cases, it was better to narrow it down to one theme. Not the five or ten themes I had received, that is for sure. Narrowing the number of themes is especially important if one's goal is to publish a compilation of stories rather than one person's life story. What I eventually realized is that I had, indeed, collected quite a number of life stories.

This advice was consistent whether the editor was more of a technical writer or more likely to work on fantasy stories. Then I began the painful process of actually cutting the stories down. No way! Is it even remotely possible? These stories had long-since become dear to my heart, which was reflected in many editorial responses during those early days. Alas, it did happen. Eventually I grew used to the new versions and realized that demonstrating one resilience theme per story worked best.

Another delay had to do with the children's stories. I went

through another pack of tissues every time I reread their stories. These stories really got to me. They are treasures of young voices; there is so much truth and wisdom in their words. The most recent reason this journey took this so long has to do with the field of publication today.

Even when I complain to my family and friends, they know that I have enjoyed this process. I have learned more than I would have ever imagined from working on each story. I have come to appreciate my own stories and my family's stories even more, many of which reflect resilience. Resilience shows up in the smallest, every day ways just as much as it does in the big picture. One small example is when one child tells another child to stand up tall as he or she heads to the front of the class to give a report. A big picture example is when my friend, who had trouble with her licensing exam the first time, pulled herself together to do it all again. Once licensed, she worked as a well-regarded therapist in a highly successful practice.

I remember a perfect example of resilience, especially of teaching it to others. A favorite principal, whose school covered a wide age range of students, used to sit outdoors in nice weather. He sat along a low brick wall, which put him at eye level with many of the students. It was common to see students stop by for a chat. This principal had a way of talking and, even more importantly, a way of listening that let the students know he was with them. He did not care if they were complaining about class, complimenting him on his new tie, asking about longer recesses and no homework days, or itching for a fight with a classmate. He soothed a lot of minds, hearts, and souls. He helped students get it together, look at things in a different way, and come up with alternate solutions. He taught resilience by example.

RECOMMENDED READING LIST

Beilock, Sian. *How the Body Knows Its Mind: The Surprising Power of the Physical Environment to Influence How You Think and Feel.* New York: Atria Paperback, An Imprint of Simon & Schuster, Inc., 2015.

Benard, Bonnie. *Resiliency: What We Have Learned.* San Francisco: WestEd, 2004.

Bloom, Paul. *Against Empathy: The Case for Rational Compassion.* New York: Ecco, An Imprint of Harper Collins Publishers, 2016.

Brett, Doris. *Annie Stories: A Special Kind of Storytelling.* New York: Workman Publishing, 1988.

Brown, Brene, Ph.D., LMSW. *Daring Greatly: How the Courage to Be Vulnerable Transforms the Way We Live, Love, Parent, and Lead.* New York: Gotham Books, Penguin Group, Inc., 2012.

—. *The Gifts of Imperfection: Let Go of Who You Think You're Supposed to Be and Embrace Who You Are.* Center City, MN: Hazelden, 2010.

Buelow, Beth L. *The Introvert Entrepreneur: Amplify Your Strengths and Create*

Success on Your Own Terms. New York: Perigee, an Imprint of Penguin Random House, 2015.

Bycel, Lee T. *Refugees in America: Stories of Courage, Resilience, and Hope, in Their Own Words*. New Brunswick, NJ: Rutgers University Press, 2019.

Cain, Susan. *Quiet: The Power of Introverts in a World That Can't Stop Talking*. New York: Crown, 2012.

Capacchione, Lucia, Ph.D. *The Creative Journal: The Art of Finding Yourself: 35th Anniversary Edition*. Athens, Ohio: Swallow Press, an imprint of Ohio University Press, 2015.

—. *The Power of Your Other Hand: A Course in Channeling the Wisdom of the Right Brain*. Pompton Plains, NJ: New Page Books/The Career Press, Inc., 2001.

Carlos, John P. and Rick Miller. *Kids at Hope: Every Child Can Succeed, No Exceptions*. Champaign,IL: Sagamore Publishing LLC, 2007.

Carroll, Andrew, Editor. *Operation Homecoming: Iraq, Afghanistan, and the Home Front, in the Words of U.S. Troops and Their Families*. New York: Random House, 2006.

Chapman, Gary, Ph.D., and Ross Campbell, M.D. *The 5 Love Languages of Children*. Chicago: Northfield Publishing, 2012.

Colgrove, Melba, Ph.D., Harold H. Bloomfield, M.D., & Peter McWilliams. *How to Survive the Loss of a Love*. 2006.

Cyrulnik, Boris. *Resilience: How Your Inner Strength Can Set You Free from the Past.* New York: MJF Books, 2011.

Dempsey, Ernest. Editor-in-Chief of Online Journal called *Recovering the Self: A Journal of Hope and Healing.* Website is www.recoveringself.com.

Doidge, Norman, M.D. *The Brain That Changes Itself: Stories of Personal Triumph from the Frontiers of Brain Science.* New York: Viking, 2007.

Duckworth, Angela. *Grit: The Power of Passion and Perseverance.* New York: Scribner, an imprint of Simon and Schuster, Inc., 2016.

Dutton, Judy. *Science Fair Season: Twelve Kids, A Robot Names Scorch and What it Takes to Win.* New York: Hyperion, 2011.

Faber, Adele and Elaine Mazlish. *How to Talk so Kids Will Listen and Listen so Kids Will Talk.* New York: Schribner, A Division of Simon & Schuster, Inc., 2012.

Fu, Ping with MeiMei Fox. *Bend, Not Break: A Life in Two Worlds.* New York: Portfolio/Penguin, 2012.

Gonzales, Laurence. *Surviving Survival: The Art and Science of Resilience.* New York: W. W. Norton & Company, 2012.

Graziano, Michael S. A. *The Spaces Between Us: A Story of Neuroscience, Evolution, and Human Nature.* New York: Oxford University Press, 2018.

Greenberg, Joanne. *I Never Promised You a Rose Garden*. New York: St. Martin's Press, 2009.

Hammond, Darell. *KABOOM! How one man built a movement to save play*. New York: Special Markets Department, Rodale Inc., 2011.

Hickam, Homer Jr. *Rocket Boys: A Memoir*. New York: Delacorte Press, Bantam Doubleday Dell Publishing Group, Inc., 1998.

Hillenbrand, Laura. *Unbroken: A World War II Story of Survival, Resilience, and Redemption*. New York: Random House, 2010.

Kenny, Deborah. *Born to Rise: A Story of Children and Teachers Reaching Their Highest Potential*. New York: Harper Collins, 2012.

Livingston, Gordon, M.D. *Too Soon Old, Too Late Smart: Thirty True Things You Need to Know Now*. New York: MJF Books, 2004.

McGonigal, Kelly, Ph.D. *The Upside of Stress: Why Stress is Good For You and How to Get Good At It*. New York: Avery, A Member of Penguin Random House, 2015.

McGowan, Chris. *Saving Science Class: Why We Need Hands-On Science to Engage Kids, Inspire Curiosity, and Improve Education*. Amherst, NY: Prometheus Publishing, 2017.

McKenzie, Richard B., Editor. *Home Away From Home: The Forgotten History of Orphanages*. New York: Encounter Books, 2009.

—. *Rethinking Orphanages for the 21ˢᵗ Century.* Thousand Oaks, CA: Sage Publications, Inc., 1999.

McKenzie, Richard. *Miracle Mountain: A Hidden Sanctuary for Children, Horses, and Birds Off a Road Less Traveled.* Irvine, CA: Dickens Press, 2013.

—. *The Home: A Memoir of Growing Up in an Orphanage.* Irvine, CA: Dickens Press, 2006.

McRaven, Admiral William H. (U.S. Navy Retired). *Make Your Bed: Little Things That Can Change Your Life...and Maybe the World.* New York: Grand Central Publishing, Hachette Book Group, 2017.

Newmark, Amy. *Chicken Soup for the Soul: Find Your Inner Strength: 101 Empowering Stories of Resilience, Positive Thinking & Overcoming Challenges.* Cos Cob, CT: Chicken Soup for the Soul Publishing, LLC, 2014.

Petersen, Andrea. *On Edge: A Journey Through Anxiety.* New York: Published by Crown, an imprint of the Crown Publishing Group, a division of Penguin Random House LLC, 2017.

Peterson, Jordan. *12 Rules for Life: An Antidote to Chaos.* Toronto: Random House Canada, a division of Penguin Random House Canada, Limited, 2018.

Pipher, Mary, Ph.D. *Reviving Ophelia: Saving the Selves of Adolescent Girls.* New York: Riverhead Books, Penguin Group, 2005.

Sacks, Oliver. *The Mind's Eye.* New York: Vintage Books, A Division of Random House Inc., 2010.

—. *Uncle Tungsten: Memories of a Chemical Boyhood.* New York: Vintage Books, A Division of Random House, Inc., 2001.

Sapolsky, Robert M. *Why Zebras Don't Get Ulcers: The Acclaimed Guide to Stress, Stress-Related Diseases, and Coping.* New York: A Holt Paperback, Henry Holt and Company, 2004.

Sax, Leonard. *The Collapse of Parenting: How We Hurt Our Kids When We Treat Them Like Grown-Ups.* New York: Basic Books, 2016.

Seligman, Martin E.P., Ph.D. *Authentic Happiness: Using the New Positive Psychology to Realize Your Potential for Lasting Fulfillment.* New York: The Free Press, A Division of Simon & Schuster, Inc., 2002.

—. *The Optimistic Child: A Proven Program to Safeguard Children Against Depression and Build Lifelong Resilience.* New York: Houghton Mifflin Company, 2007.

Shapiro, Francine. *Getting Past Your Past: Take Control of Your Life with Self-Help Techniques from EMDR Therapy.* Emmaus, PA: Rodale, 2012.

Siebert, Al, Ph.D. *The Resiliency Advantage: Master Change, Thrive Under Pressure, and Bounce Back From Setbacks.* San Francisco: Berrett-Koehler Publishers, Inc., 2005.

Siegel, Daniel J., M.D. *Brainstorm: The Power and Purpose of the Teenage Brain.* New York: Jeremy P. Tarcher/Penguin, 2015.

—. *Mindsight: The New Science of Personal Transformation.* New

York: Bantam Books, an imprint of The Random House Publishing Group, 2010.

Silverstein, Ken. *The Radioactive Boy Scout*. New York: Villard Books, 2005.

Simpson, Joe. *Touching the Void: The True Story of One Man's Miraculous Survival*. New York: Perennial, an Imprint of Harper Collins, 2004.

Sundlun, Kara. *Finding Dad: From Love Child to Daughter*. Burlington, Iowa: Behler Publications, 2015.

Tough, Paul. *How Children Succeed: Grit, Curiosity, and the Hidden Power of Character*. New York: Mariner Books, Houghton Mifflin Harcourt, 2012.

Van der Kolk, Bessel, Ph.D. *The Body Keeps the Score: Train, Mind, and Body in the Healing of Trauma*. New York: Viking, Penguin Group LLC, 2014.

Weir, Andy. *The Martian*. New York: Crown Publishers, an imprint of the Crown

Publishing Group, a division of Random House LLC, a Penguin Random House Company, 2014.

Werner, Emmy E. *A Conspiracy of Decency: The Rescue of the Danish Jews During World War II*. Boulder, CO: Westview Press, A Member of the Perseus Book Group, 2002.

—. *Through the Eyes of Innocents: Children Witness World War II*.

Boulder, CO: Westview Press, A Member of the Perseus Book Group, 2000.

Werner, Emmy E., and Ruth S. Smith. *Journeys from Childhood to Midlife: Risk, Resilience, and Recovery.* Ithaca, NY: Cornell University Press, 2001.

—. *Overcoming the Odds: High Risk Children from Birth to Adulthood.* Ithaca, NY: Cornell University Press, 1993.

ACKNOWLEDGMENTS

Thank you to every person who helped with this book—to name everyone individually would prove more than difficult. First, thank you to my family members for their continued encouraging words, no matter how many times they repeated them over recent years. While contributing to the book's clarity, my spouse's red pen has run out of ink many times. Another important contribution from my spouse was offering to make dinner, asking how about turning the computer off, and suggesting we go for a hike, a drive, or shopping now and then.

Others to thank are out-of-state friends who spent way more than the allotted time on the phone, texting, and emailing with ideas and encouragement every day of the week. I want to thank graduate school and private practice friends, especially my two closest ones, who helped every step of the way. They never let me get discouraged. This meant a lot in keeping me going and in starting over as needed.

My current editor prefers to 'work behind the scenes.' She has been a great support, offered creative ideas, and conveyed words of wisdom about organization and sentence structure. I cannot imagine completing this book without her. Local friends have been immensely supportive, as I have executed restart after restart and phone call after phone call. Thank you all. Special thanks go to my game night friends, to one close friend who has shared a multitude of exercise classes with me, and to certain university instructors who taught those classes. Your confidence in me and in the value of this book has been a blessing. This book would still be flailing around without the inspiration of my coffee friends—thanks to each one of you.

ABOUT THE AUTHOR

Alex Prescott Hartwell worked part time as a licensed marriage and family therapist for a number of years, co-founded a small private practice with colleagues and friends, and worked primarily with adults. The author received advanced training in several areas and helped clients with concerns including life transitions, grief processing, educational matters, and relationship issues.

Hartwell worked in education as well, engaged fulltime in a many-year career that involved teaching a variety of students, including just about every unique and individual category known in the field of education. The work occurred in different states and covered the age range from four to twenty-one over the whole time. At times, this work also included program development.

Hartwell's keen interest in how individuals face difficulties and solve problems led to this first book. The author currently resides in western Colorado.

Lightning Source UK Ltd.
Milton Keynes UK
UKHW010418091220
374864UK00001B/39